"They must be among the most intimidating words Jesus ever spoke: 'I tell you, on the day of judgment people will give account for every careless word they speak . . .' Each one of us is responsible for our every word. In an age of ubiquitous and lightning-fast communication, we need to hear and heed this warning like never before, and for that reason, I'm thankful for Daniel Darling's call for both responsibility and civility in every word we speak—not to mention every word we write, blog, or tweet."

Tim Challies, blogger at challies.com and author of *The Discipline of Discernment*

"Online interactions shape and impact all of our lives, and yet there are so few helpful, biblical guides on how to have healthy online conversations. Fortunately, Daniel Darling has written just that. *A Way with Words* is a timely resource for those of us who find ourselves utilizing email and social media to work, learn, or keep up with friends and family. Dan writes with humility, wit and a gospel-centered perspective, making this a valuable read."

JD Greear, pastor of Summit Church and author of *What Are You Going to Do with Your Life?* and *Above All*

"*A Way with Words* offers much-needed wisdom and practical counsel on one of today's greatest discipleship challenges: our behavior online."

Thomas S. Kidd, author of *Who Is an Evangelical? The History of a Movement in Crisis*

"This is not just a book about words, but a book about the weight and power of words—and how we use them. *A Way with Words* ought to be required reading for all who enter the public square, whether as professionals, pundits, armchair theologians, or merely social media users—that is to say, all of us. Dan Darling is always wise and always pastoral. This book is Dan Darling at his best."

Karen Swallow Prior, author of *On Reading Well: Finding the Good Life through Great Books* and *Fierce Convictions: The Extraordinary Life of Hannah More—Poet, Reformer, Abolitionist*

"Talk on the internet so easily makes us into our worst selves. Thank God, then, for Daniel Darling's incisive new book about the problems we make for ourselves. His thoughts on discernment show both humble self-examination and careful observation, not to mention pastoral sensitivity. Highly recommended for any Christian looking for guidance through the rocky terrain of online discourse!"

David Zahl, author of *Seculosity* and editor of The Mockingbird Blog

A WAY WITH

WORDS

A WAY WITH
WORDS

USING OUR
ONLINE
CONVERSATIONS
FOR GOOD

DANIEL DARLING

B&H
PUBLISHING
NASHVILLE, TENNESSEE

To all those who have nurtured my writing life:

—Mrs. Birginal for telling an awkward junior high boy that he had talent
—My father for constantly telling me I'd be a writer one day
—My first boss, Julie Dearyan, for pushing me to get published
—My mentor, Bill Swanger, for reminding me that writing is a ministry

Acknowledgments

This is my ninth published book and I don't take any of this for granted. To have anyone publish your work at any level is a privilege and not a right. So first and foremost I'm thankful to Taylor Combs for seeing the vision behind this book and to B&H for publishing it. Every decision a publisher makes is a risk, and I want to thank B&H for taking this one on with me. The entire team at B&H has made this a wonderful writing process from idea to editing to publishing to marketing.

I'm also indebted to my agent, Erik Wolgemuth, who has been a wonderful guide in this writing journey. Thanks for fielding all my ideas, rapid-fire, even when many of them are not good.

I'm thankful for the wonderful friends I have at ERLC, where I was privileged to work for six years, especially Dr. Russell Moore for allowing me to serve alongside in helping us help Christians think well about the culture. I grew so much at ERLC and my writing ministry flourished there.

I'm thankful for my new colleagues, especially Troy Miller, at NRB, where we are helping to shape the next generation of Christian communicators.

I'm thankful for my pastor, Daryl Crouch, who encourages me in this and every endeavor.

Last, my wife Angela has been an indispensable and life-giving partner on this journey. And to my kids: thanks for putting up with Dad hunched over his laptop looking off, eyes glazed, into the distance while gathering another writing thought. This is why.

Contents

A Book about Words

"I know nothing in the world that has as much power as a word. Sometimes I write one, and I look at it until it begins to shine."
—Emily Dickinson

'll never forget hearing my oldest daughter, Grace, speak her first words. Angela and I and our family on both sides had waited so long for the moment her verbal communication rose above grunts and animal sounds to something resembling what humans speak. *What would she say? How would it sound? Would she talk at all?*

Like most first-time parents we worried irrationally, consulting baby books, our pediatrician, and other parents. Google was a bit rudimentary back then but I'm sure we also consulted the search engine for help.

Eventually Grace did speak, and her first word wasn't "mommy" or even "daddy." It was the simple, but rather effective, "No!"

Chasing Words

Hearing Grace speak was a joy, even if the words that came from her mouth were, even at her vulnerable age, a testament to her strong will and her independence. They excited me as they would excite any parent hearing their kid speak for the first time, but perhaps more for me because I've spent a lifetime chasing words.

My mother taught me to read at an early age, and I've been devouring words ever since. We took three newspapers at our house: the *Daily Herald,* the *Chicago Tribune,* and the *Chicago Sun Times.* I read them every day. Sports first, then news, then features. On Sundays I spread out those gloriously fat Sunday editions and was silent for hours.

I regularly visited libraries, begged my mother to buy more Hardy Boys and Nancy Drew books, and, at times, read the ingredients on the cereal boxes when there was nothing left in our house to read. My parents, because they feared the influence of television, didn't own a set until I was in college, so it was either listening to words on the radio or reading them on a page.

But not only have I read words, I've been stringing them together from a very young age (albeit not always very well). In junior high, a teacher made an offhand comment that set a trajectory for the rest of my life. She told me, after reviewing some essays I'd written for English literature, "Dan, I think you have a gift. You should pursue writing."

Those words changed my life. I saw myself as a writer from that very moment. It didn't hurt that my father, a man of few words, frequently whispered to me, "Dan, you are going to be a famous writer one day."

I'm not famous, but by God's grace in directing my crooked steps, I've been writing professionally for almost two decades. I've served in a variety of roles—editor, pastor, executive—but in every position I've brought with me my love for words. I'm just not good at anything else. I can't dance. I can't weld. I can't make an omelet. Words are what I love.

I feel a lot like George Will, who confessed once that he didn't know what he'd be doing if he wasn't writing, or like the novelist Ray Bradbury, who said once, "I don't need an alarm clock. My ideas wake me."

These days, that's happening more and more often. And until someone tells me I can't write words, I'm going to keep writing them.

Now, I imagine you may not be as obsessed with words as I am, and that's quite all right. God has likely given you other loves, other pursuits that awaken your soul and give you joy. But I might say that even if you are not a writer like me in search of the perfect word, you should care about words, and more important, the way you use them—both in your everyday conversation and, in the case of this book, the way we so often deploy them: online.

A Speaking God and Speaking Humans

In *The Dignity Revolution*, I explored what it means to be created *imago dei*, that is, "in the image of God." I continue to be fascinated by the rich language the Bible uses to describe humanity. God spoke into existence all of creation, but Moses pauses his narrative in the first two chapters to make a statement about the intricate detail God uses to create men and women. God, Moses says, reached with his hands and crafted humans from the dust of the ground and breathed into humans the breath of life (Gen. 2:7).

It's a beautiful mystery, this idea of being a reflection of the divine. And there is much wrapped in what *imago dei* means. But one of the key ways we reflect God is that we, of all creatures, are communicating beings. We use words.

Christianity is, after all, a religion that believes in a speaking God. We sometimes take this for granted, casually saying things like, "God told me to take that job," but we don't often enough stop and marvel that God speaks.

He is not obligated to speak, and yet he does. You could argue, as Timothy Ward does effectively in his excellent book *Words of Life,* that speaking is at the heart of God's self-revelation. "It is often observed that God's words and actions are intimately related in the Bible. To say of God that he spoke, and to say of God that he did something, is often one and the same thing . . . He is a God who by his very nature acts by speaking."[1] Ward is exactly right. We know of God only because he has chosen to speak.

I still marvel that after Adam and Eve fell in the garden, God went after them. So invested was he in his image-bearers that he . . . spoke to them: "Where are you?" (Gen. 3:9). This is such divine grace. Ward says that God "speaking is also an integral part of God acting to save."[2]

In fact, you could argue that the storyline of Scripture—God's own revealed Word to us—is a narrative of God speaking. Just think, for instance, how often the Old Testament contains the phrase, "and the word of the LORD came to . . ." The prophets were always speaking because they first heard God speak.

And in the New Testament, the coming of Jesus is framed by John as what? The Word made flesh (John 1). Even the flesh-and-blood incarnation is God communicating to his people. In other words, God doesn't just speak words; in Christ, we are told he *is* the Word. Jesus is the living and breathing, flesh-and-blood communication of God:

> Long ago God spoke to the fathers by the prophets at different times and in different ways. In these last days, he has spoken to us by his Son. God has appointed him heir of all things and made the universe through him. The Son is the radiance of God's glory and the exact expression of his nature, sustaining all things by his powerful word. (Heb. 1:1–3)

God speaks through Moses and the prophets and, in the new covenant (an agreement framed by words), by Jesus, whose words, he says, are the very power that both created and sustains the universe. We have, very much so, a speaking God.

Which means that those who bear his image are also speakers.[3]

Animals might communicate in a rudimentary way. A dog may signal to us that it has to go out by barking. An ape might be able to learn some kinds of sign language. And a parrot can mimic the four-letter words of its master. But creative communication, forming words, is distinctly human.

You'll never see an elephant writing a novel or an aardvark reading Chaucer. To further belabor this point, consider how our best art tries to humanize the animal kingdom—by making them speak as humans. Isn't this what makes Mickey Mouse and Donkey from *Shrek* and Mufasa from *The Lion King* so lovable? Words are what bring life to the beasts in Narnia and why Tolkien made the birds and beasts talk in *The Hobbit*. We make animals speak because words make the subhuman human.

Forming words and sentences is so woven into the human experience that we lament when a person loses this ability. We grieve when a singer loses her vocal cords or when Alzheimer's or some other form of dementia keeps a beloved author from writing. And we compensate for those who have been born without the ability to vocally pronounce words. Sign language allows people to still express themselves in rich ways, and braille and audiobooks allow the blind to consume words without seeing them.

The restoration of communication is often seen in Scripture as a sign of God's restoration in Jesus' new inaugurated kingdom activity. Christ's ministry was a fulfillment of the promise to, in part, make the mute speak (Isa. 35:4–7; Mark 7:31–37). A restoration of our image-bearing, God-reflecting ability to creatively communicate is part of Christ's new-creation work.

This is true not only on the micro level but on the macro level. Where God's judgment at the Tower of Babel meant people would be *divided* by language, the promise of Pentecost means that, in Christ, God is creating a new people who, while speaking different languages, would communicate ultimately in the new language of heaven, gathered around Jesus' throne at the end of the age, representing every tongue (Rev. 7:9). And one of the most powerful ways we express our worship is by singing and shouting praise.

You could say, without exaggeration, that God is a speaking God who loves words.

Words Gone Wild

But alas, not all the words that humans create reflect God's own beautiful words. And that's the reason for this book.

It is a bit ironic that the human race's descent into darkness began with the serpent's own twisted misrepresentation of God's words of instruction to his image-bearers. Words, after humanity's fall into sin, can now be used either to injure or inspire. This is why King David prayed that the words of his mouth be "acceptable" in the sight of God (Ps. 19:14). In a fallen world, we often don't even understand the weight of what we say or, in this age, what we type.

David's son, Solomon, understood well the power of words. The wisest man in all the world often reflected on language in his proverbs:

> There is one whose rash words are like
>   sword thrusts,
> but the tongue of the wise brings healing.
>   (Prov. 12:18 ESV)

> Death and life are in the power of the
>   tongue,
> and those who love it will eat its fruits.
>   (Prov. 18:21)

"Death and life are in the power of the tongue." And, we might say today, the power of the thumb. Words can create or destroy, they can uplift or condemn. They can reflect the Word by which God has spoken or they can echo the whispers of the serpent. So powerful are words, the apostle James tells Christian leaders, that "no one can tame" them (James 3:8).

If Solomon saw fit to warn the people of God in the Old Testament of the power of words, and if James saw fit to warn the early church of the power of words, how much more today should God's people heed what God is speaking to us about how we speak? We live in a world with a vast and seemingly unlimited economy of words. There are more ways to communicate today than at any time in human history.

It may seem at times that stewarding our communication, especially the easy and free way we communicate online, is next to impossible. We might say with James, "Who can tame this beast?" But we should remember that those destructive half-truths in the garden of Eden were not the final word. Jesus, God's Final Word, has spoken a word over those who have turned to him in faith. He declares in his Word that we are justified and we are transformed. Jesus has conquered that unruly, death-dealing beast and has given us God's Holy Spirit to help us tame our tongues and our thumbs.

In the pages that follow, we will be less interested in litigating screen time and algorithms—though that is a discussion worth having. Instead, we will consider the inevitable task of communicating in the internet age. Incivility has been with us since Eden, but the immediacy and availability of digital platforms seems to exacerbate this temptation. Alan Jacobs is right when he says the farther humans get away from face-to-face conversations, the greater the opportunity for sinful speech. Today, that distance is even more pronounced, as we can spar back and forth with complete strangers, whom we know only by an avatar. "Technologies of communication that allow us to overcome the distances of space also allow us to neglect the common humanity we share with the people we now find inhabiting our world,"[4] Jacobs writes. I don't think the mediums are always value-neutral.

Christians who believe in original sin can't quite get away with blaming Twitter and Facebook and Instagram and any other platforms—as if we are helpless in this digital age and as if the way we communicate doesn't originate from within.

Jesus reminds us, "Out of the abundance of the heart [the] mouth speaks" (Luke 6:45 ESV) . . . or the thumbs tweet, record, or post.

This will be a book asking questions about the way we conduct ourselves in this new reality, the way we behave online. The internet is not going away any time soon. Platforms may change, but the call for Christians to steward their words well is the same as it was in the beginning. May we see a revolution of kindness, so that we may pray with Paul, "Let [our] speech always be gracious" (Col. 4:6).

Chapter 1

Ever Learning, Never Arriving

*. . . always learning and never able to
come to a knowledge of the truth.*
—2 Timothy 3:7

Until recently, I had a pretty good relationship with sleep. I didn't need much of it, and when I did go to bed, I didn't have a hard time falling asleep. But as my thirties turned into forties, sleep has come a lot harder. I'm not sure why—perhaps stress, perhaps mulling over that last argument with my wife, perhaps the tumbler of ideas that are always rattling through my head. It's hard, these days, to turn off the thinker.

I have found that if I read before bed, I go to sleep much easier. There is something about a singular focus on one activity that helps prepare me for night. So lately I've made an intentional choice to read three or four chapters of a book at night. And I've taken to putting my phone across the room, to avoid the temptation to roll over and scroll endlessly.

Except that I have four wonderful children who frequently wake me up in the middle of the night.

We are in the season of parenting our four wonderful children where middle-of-the-night leg pain is frequent. The doctors tell us these are growing pains, but at the rate at which my kids wake us up with these aches, I'm starting to wonder if all of them might not end up tall enough to play professional basketball.

Typically Angela and I both wake up, but while I privately grouse about loss of sleep, she actually gets out of bed and offers the typical remedies of warm washcloths and liquid ibuprofen. On rare occasions my crankiness meets my conscience and I am the caring parent attending to midnight maladies.

But once I'm up I've found it hard to go back to sleep. So one of my temptations is to grab that glowing receptacle from its charger on the way back from a kids' bedroom and then use my collection of unread articles and Google searches on things of interest to pass the time in the wee hours. "You need to put that thing away and just go to sleep," my wife will often wisely say in a typically futile attempt to talk sense into me.

I've also reached for my phone on the occasional night when I'm restless, when a pressing issue or stress keeps me from closing my eyes. And after a fitful night, the next morning I always wonder why it is that I look to this endless portal of knowing called the internet to comfort my troubled, unquiet soul.

The Beginning of Knowledge and the End of Knowing

I'm not anti-iPhone, and this is not a book, as I said in the introduction, that is going to help you navigate screen time. But this is a book about words on the internet, and we do have to reckon with the way that we've virtually eliminated awkward quietness with an endless array of ways to occupy our brains.

It isn't just in the night watches where we are tempted to turn to the internet for more information. Ever been in a long meeting and you have that itch to grab your phone and get "caught up" on what is going on in the world? Ever been on a family vacation where you've left your phone in your room on purpose and spent hours at the pool, only to try to invent reasons to sneak back in and check Twitter? Ever work on a book project like this one you are reading and have to fight the urge to pop into Facebook?

If you aren't marking these questions with the hand-raised emoji, you should at least be silently doing this in your mind. According to a recent survey conducted by the American Psychological Association, 41 percent of Americans admit to being "compulsive phone checkers."[1] Why can't we resist this impulse? Why are we so willing to forgo the rich conversations in the room for the fleeting comments online with people we don't even know or don't even like?

The pull toward the phone often begins with good intentions—with a desire to know more. We can gain some level of knowledge about our country's political situation by reading that article we bookmarked, or garner information about work by checking email. We can get caught up on the day's events by scrolling through our Twitter feed or learn whose birthday it is by checking Facebook.

This pull toward information is natural. Christians believe that God created human beings to pursue knowledge of him and of his world. This is inherent in the divine instructions given to Adam and Eve in the garden to cultivate the earth. King David describes, for instance, the way even the natural world pulls at our senses and leads us into an exploration of the unknown:

> The heavens declare the glory of God, and the expanse proclaims the work of his hands. Day after day they pour out speech; night after night they communicate knowledge. (Ps. 19:1–2)

The heavens, he writes, *pour out knowledge.*

> There is no speech; there are no words; their voice is not heard. Their message has gone out to the whole earth, and their words to the ends of the world. (Ps. 19:3–4)

In other words, the world and everything in it have messages to be heard, even if there are no words. Trees aren't writing sentences and oceans aren't forming paragraphs, and yet in a way, they are, because creation can't help but speak volumes about the Creator.

You can't live as a creature in God's world without the pursuit of knowledge. It's impossible. The natural world is layered with information, shouting out to those who seek after God. This is why even secular scientists would admit that humans have only but scratched the surface of what is to be explored and known. There are untold wonders around the universe yet to be discovered.

And not only is it impossible to not be always learning, acquiring knowledge is something essential to human flourishing. Listen to the way the one who resists knowledge is mocked in Proverbs:

> How long, inexperienced ones, will you love
>   ignorance?
> How long will you mockers enjoy mocking
>   and you fools hate knowledge? (1:22)

To despise knowledge is to work against our own flourishing and to resist the way we were created by God to know and be known. And to pursue knowledge is to be enriched "with every precious and beautiful treasure" (Prov. 24:4). "Because they hated knowledge," another proverb reads, they "don't choose to fear the LORD" (1:29). To love God fully, Jesus reminded us, quoting from the Law, is to love with our minds (Matt. 22:37–40).

You don't have to be a Christian like me to get this. Almost every sociological study affirms that education is a key factor in helping people move from poverty to purpose. And we should be grateful for the way technology has made knowledge much easier to access for the most vulnerable in ways that could only be dreamed of in almost every other era of human history.

I try to make this point with my kids. They think I'm a fossil when I tell them that when I was a kid there was no internet. *Really, Dad?* Yes, really. We had to get our parents to drive us to the library so we could work on that project for school. And yet I remember the rush of excitement when I got access to that micro-film and back issues of periodicals like *Newsweek* and *Time*. I remember specifically preparing a presentation on Watergate where I found countless magazine and newspaper articles. I remember being overwhelmed about the vastness of the information in our local library.

We still take our kids to the library and, thankfully, they think it's awesome. But their first instinct when they need to know some information is to Google it or, even easier, to ask Alexa.

Having access to seemingly unlimited stores of information is, I think, a net good. Think of all the ways that lives are saved, that connections are made, that ordinary things in life have just been made easier because of the digital age.

The internet can help us find a church, connect with long-lost friends, and in many cases, help people find spouses and get married. The internet can help ignite important social movements, can keep us from getting lost in an unfamiliar location, and can give access to life-saving medical information.

As a Christian, I can and should applaud the progress of this digital age as a sign of humanity's ability to create from the raw materials of God's good creation. And yet, we have to acknowledge the downside, in a fallen world, of having so much information at our fingertips and the temptations this knowledge invites.

There is a way to pursue knowledge that leads away from flourishing and can lead us away from the source of our knowledge, God himself.

In his last New Testament letter, the apostle Paul, a well-educated, lifelong learner, warned his young protégé Timothy about a pursuit of knowledge that is "always learning and never able to come to a knowledge of the truth" (2 Tim. 3:7).

This, I believe, is what separates a genuine hunger for knowledge with a never-ending, insatiable thirst for knowing. There is a difference between a curious mind and a meandering heart.

The internet can make us smarter, but it can also be the equivalent of eating junk food three meals a day. Christians who live in this age have to resist the wrong impulses of either being drawn into endless rabbit trails of information or withdrawing completely.[2]

Information discipline begins, I believe, by getting to the heart of why we pick up our phones and why we often mindlessly hit "search" or why we give in to another guilty click on a click-baity article on a celebrity breakup. What is at the heart of our endless need to check in on social media, our never-ending Google searches for fruitless information, and our restlessness in this age of information?

With most questions, I'm drawn back to the very beginning of the Bible, to the story that Christianity tells about the nature of humanity and the character of God. God planted the first humans in a garden rich with sensory experiences and urged them to pursue knowledge and cultivate his good creation. But there was a tree, aptly named, I believe, the tree of the knowledge of good and evil. On first blush, it's hard for us to understand why God would not want his image-bearers to know good and evil. Isn't knowledge a means of human flourishing in a world where God's creation shouts information?

This question, actually, frames the serpent's appeal to Eve: *Why would God, if he is a good Father, keep this information from you? The fruit you are forbidden to eat tastes good but, more important, it will lift you to vistas of knowledge you don't have now, data that God, if he were good, would not withhold from you.*

But could there be a kind of knowing that is not good for us, that undermines our quest for true wisdom? Jen Pollack Michel writes that what Satan was getting at was not knowledge itself, but a false promise that "one could have the infinite, infallible, wisdom of God."[3] When I first read this in her book, *Surprised by Paradox,* I had to read it again several times. Because this is exactly, I think, the great temptation of the digital age.

Let me explain by sharing more of my own vulnerabilities. I've always had a curious mind. Ever since I was a child, I've been reading. Newspapers. Books. Magazines. And now, of course, online publications, email newsletters, tweets.

There is a joy in learning that I hope stays with me for my whole life, but there is also a subtle sense of control—of being my own god—that I feel when I have my phone. One of the lies my phone tells me is that I don't actually need God. I can control my life and my destiny and the well-being of my family and friends because with this digital device, I have access to power. I can text powerful people. I can tweet and grow my audience. I can fire off an email to my staff and set things in motion. And even when I'm in a crowd of people that I'm not that familiar with, I can do some quick Google and Wikipedia searches and get up to speed on conversations.

Ironically, I don't actually walk around thinking, "I'm powerful. I'm a god. I don't need God." It's subconscious. But do you know when I feel this most acutely? When, for some reason, I'm disconnected.

When I'm in a meeting where I can't get away with sneaking peeks at social media. When I'm in an Uber in a city I don't know and my phone is dead. When I finally set my phone down on the charger and walk that ten feet to my bed, absent from the world.

It's an interesting thing. When I'm connected to my phone, I often feel I don't need God because I feel like a god. When I'm disconnected from my phone, I know I need God because I feel like a creature. I recognize that I'm human, completely dependent on him.

My worst experience was the time my phone was unable to connect to Verizon. This lasted for about two days. I could hook up to Wi-Fi, so while at work I could get texts and check email and social media, but in the car rides in between work and home, I was unplugged. It all sounds so pathetic, I know, but it's real. I felt a loss of control. I couldn't find the fastest way home via Waze; I had to just take the standard route. I couldn't listen to my favorite podcasts. I couldn't even call home.

For thirty minutes, I was not in control of my life. I could not seek new information. I couldn't master my world. And I didn't like it.

Maybe your world is not as wrapped around your phone as mine seems to be. But at some level you see the ways the digital age and it's promise of omniscience tug at your soul. Can you see that there is a way of knowing that is not about growing and learning and ultimately finding it's way, our way, to the truth and to the Author of truth but is instead a desire to "be in the know" and, in subtle ways, to be God instead of merely imaging him?

If, as Proverbs 1:7 tells us, "the fear of the LORD is the beginning of knowledge," a healthy perspective recognizes that there are limits to what we can know. We are not God. We are not the source of all things.

To be God, to be the infinite source of all things, was the temptation the serpent laid before Eve. The fruit offered to Eve the illusion of control. It's a short-sighted trade-off, really, exchanging your status as image-bearers pursuing knowledge that leads to great intimacy with the One who made you for a vain attempt to be the source of all things. This is the seductive lie whispered to us in the dark watches of the night, or during a boring meeting, or while in conversation with a rambling neighbor. We're missing out, we think, on an all-knowing that the internet promises to deliver.

Eve, you might say, experienced in a less digital way the first FOMO.[4] FOMO is the cold fear that there is something going on in the world about which we are not privy, an experience we are not at the center of. A world we cannot control.

How to Know Well

One response would be to completely pull back: chuck our smartphones, smash our laptops, and make our televisions less smart. Perhaps, for some, drastic measures like this might be needed. If your right eye offend, cut it out, Jesus says in Matthew 5:29.

And yet even these drastic measures do not help us answer the question of what fuels our FOMO. Dave Zahl says that "the problem is not information on its own but the accompanying imperative about staying abreast of it all, which is fed, presumably, by the need to master, to prove our relevance, to justify our existence. Technology has just made the pursuit more convenient."[5]

This "imperative to stay abreast of it all," this longing to never miss any breaking news story or juicy gossip or titillating conversation is, I think, what Paul is getting at when he condemns "busybodies," both in his letter to the believers at Thessalonica (2 Thess. 3:11) and to Timothy (1 Tim. 5:13). Paul was not against the pursuit of wisdom and knowledge. All over his letters, we see him urge people to study and grow and learn. And it is Paul who, nearing his own death, asked for someone to bring his books (2 Tim. 4:13). And yet he understood the difference between idle pursuit of cheap information and a lifelong commitment to wisdom. He committed to this discipline in his own life, telling the church at Corinth that he "decided to know nothing among you except Jesus Christ and him crucified" (1 Cor. 2:2).

Christians are not called to simply have curious minds but disciplined, renewed minds (Rom. 12:2). And there is growing evidence among those who study the brain that the flashes of data we consume here and there in our daily obsession with checking in on the world through social media can rob us of real, genuine learning. Back in 2008, Nicholas Carr wrote a penetrating essay that later became a 2012 book, *The Shallows.* Carr noticed the way his reading on the internet—the skimming we all do—was diminishing his capacity for deep knowledge and reflection.

> For more than a decade now, I've been spending a lot of time online, searching and surfing and sometimes adding to the great databases of the Internet. The Web has been a godsend to me as a writer. . . . Even when I'm not working, I'm as likely as not to be foraging in the Web's info-thickets, reading and writing e-mails, scanning headlines and blog posts, watching videos and listening to podcasts, or just tripping from link to link to link. . . .
>
> The advantages of having immediate access to such an incredibly rich store of information are many, and they've been widely described and duly applauded. . . . But that boon comes at a price. . . . And what the Net seems to be doing is chipping away my capacity for concentration and contemplation. My mind now expects to take in information the way the

Net distributes it: in a swiftly moving stream
of particles. Once I was a scuba diver in the
sea of words. Now I zip along the surface like
a guy on a Jet Ski.[6]

This essay was written in 2008, more than a decade ago
and before social media usage became such a regular part of
our lives. Like Carr, I've spent much of the last two decades
online as part of my work as a writer and speaker. Having
access to everything has been essential to my work, even
in writing this very chapter. And yet we have to recognize
what Carr has exposed and what the apostle Paul seems to be
getting at: there is a difference between a fruitless quest for
knowledge and a desire to be formed by intentional, forma-
tional pursuits of wisdom and knowledge.

There are practical ways to combat this desire to be "in
the know" all the time, to avoid the busybody mentality that
always tempts. Personally, besides my discipline of not having my phone by my bed, I've found marking out intentional
times for reading has kept me from the impulse to be in the
social-media fray. I also try to ask myself if what I'm reading
online—whether I'm enjoying it or not—is worth my time.
Quite often I use the "read later" feature on my internet
browser instead of reading a link that someone has tweeted
right away. I'm surprised how less interested I am in someone's "hot take" a few days later when that take has cooled
off considerably.

I've also intentionally purchased a Kindle that only allows
me to read books. No social media apps or other distractions.

And while I prefer to read paper books, I've found I consume bigger books and spend longer times reading when I'm using a Kindle, perhaps because I can see my progress at the bottom or because it is lit in a way that doesn't hurt my eyes.

Still, the seduction of the shallows of all-knowing tempt me every day. This is why those of us who spend a lot of time online because of our vocations must prioritize local, offline community with people disconnected from the hurly-burly of the internet.

Ultimately what keeps me from an "ever learning" that pulls me away from a pursuit of God is to commit to regular spiritual disciplines. I'm happy to report that now, when I have sleepless nights, I've been better at turning those moments to prayer. Some of my best times with the Lord have been those wee hours of the morning when I can't go sleep. I'm not perfect, and I will still have occasional moments when I'll walk across the room, in the dark, to pick up my phone, like an addict taking one more hit. But it always leaves me feeling empty. And I find myself, still, scrolling instead of being fully present in meetings. The struggle is real.

I have noticed a correlation in my own life between frivolous time online and prayerlessness, a phenomenon Tony Reinke notes in his book, *Competing Spectacles*:

> Prayerlessness may be the fault of my media. It is certainly the fault of my heart. In the little cracks of time in my day, with the limited attention, I am more apt to check or feed social media than I am to pray. Because of my

negligence, God grows increasingly distant from my life.[7]

Prayer frees us from FOMO, the busybody life. It is liberating when we realize that the burden of all-knowing is one we were never meant to bear, one we can resist and let go as we rest in the joy of knowing God and being known by him.[8] The serpent's lie doesn't lead us toward joy but toward a restless life of wanting, but never finding, control. God, in Christ, offers us a deep rest. We don't have to worry about missing a conversation or a conflict. We can lay down the futile attempt to be the most informed person in the room. Because the quick thrill of being in the know is a cheap substitute for the peace of knowing the One who created us and rescues us from our fruitless pursuits and is leading us toward a place where our longings to know and be known will be fully realized.

The real pursuit of wisdom begins by understanding that there is One who not only knows more than we do, but knows us by name.

Chapter 2

Slow to Tweet, Quick to Listen, Quick to Get the Whole Story

My dear brothers and sisters, understand
this: Everyone should be quick to listen,
slow to speak, and slow to anger.
—James 1:19

ominique Moran's life was nearly destroyed by the internet. One moment she was a college student from California working at a Minnesota Chipotle to help pay her way through college. And in another moment she was a symbol of systemic racism, universally condemned on social media, covered by major news networks, and fired from her job. The video of her supposed misdeeds was viewed by seven million people.

The only problem? Moran, a Mexican-American, didn't do anything that the digital mob claimed she did.

It all happened at the end of her shift one night, when a group of rowdy young men came into Chipotle, phone cameras rolling. Recognizing two of the boys, she reminded them that if they were going to order food, they'd have to pay for it. Previously they'd tried to "dine and dash." Other area restaurants in the area reported similar incidents. But this context, this detail, escaped the online mobs who rushed to create a villain out of Moran after one of the young men posted the video on social media. It served as confirmation that Moran—misidentified by the online crowd as white—was just one more racist stereotyping minority customers. Moran, who had no social media profiles at the time, was unaware of her swirling controversy. But the next day she was awakened by a phone call from her mother and instantly became aware of her newfound infamy.

Her life would never be the same. Not only was Dominique fired from her job, she received ugly death threats. One commenter promised to burn her grandmother and send the body to Moran in a bag. In less than twenty-four hours, she went from obscure, ordinary college student to worldwide villain. She said, "I felt embarrassed. Nobody wants to be called a racist in front of the world."[1] For Moran, a minority and a devoted follower of Christ, this brought feelings of guilt. *Maybe this is true about me,* she started to wonder.

There are awful pockets of ugly racism throughout our country and too many incidents where black and brown people are stereotyped by institutions that should know better. But what happens when someone is falsely accused of something so heinous?

Thankfully, for Moran, a minority herself, there was another Christian who refused to run with the reigning narrative and closely analyzed the video posted by the kids who entered that Chipotle. Andrew Hallwarth realized that there had to be more to the story, so he investigated and began to question the story on Twitter. Soon people began to rally to Dominique's side. But while her reputation has improved, her life will never be the same.

This is just one of so many stories where overreacting online helps create false narratives and gather mobs in ways that can permanently destroy reputations.

As I read this story, I was most haunted by the way one journalist ends his write-up:

> There is another question that gnaws at her as well: When a crime is committed, someone is supposed to pay. But where is justice for me?
>
> She has received no apologies from any member of the internet mob that stalked her.
>
> No contrition from the anonymous commentators, who branded her a racist, called her names and threatened her safety.[2]

No justice. No apologies. No contrition.

Confirmation Bias and the Hive Mind

If you are reading this book, you probably don't consider yourself someone eager to join a mob and ruin someone's life. But it is so easy to do. Today's mobs are not found on the street with sticks and stones; they are dressed nicely in office cubicles, sitting quietly in church pews, and sipping coffee in the comfort of air-conditioned homes. The mobs are . . . us.

Every person who tweeted or posted or Instagrammed about Dominique Moran, in a split-second expression of disgust at what they perceived as racism based on an out-of-context video didn't sign up to be part of a mob and, with few exceptions, probably didn't intend to hurt someone. And yet, they did. While I didn't join the fracas with this particular story, I've angrily posted about other perceived outrages well before I knew the facts. I thought I was right. And even if I was, was it right to join the shame chorus?

Rod Dreher reminds us that "a mob that is on the side of justice is no less a mob. I have felt that rage too, and it's *intoxicating.*"[3]

It is intoxicating. So intoxicating that we are tempted to immediately post something without stopping to consider if what we are communicating is true. And we often fail, in these split-second decisions, to consider the humanity of the person or organization we are joining a mob to crush.

Why does this happen? If we were honest, we do this because we *want* certain things to be true. Experts call this tendency "confirmation bias." One expert defines it this way:

> Confirmation bias occurs from the direct influence of desire on beliefs. When people would like a certain idea or concept to be true, they end up believing it to be true. They are motivated by wishful thinking. This error

leads the individual to stop gathering information when the evidence gathered so far
confirms the views or prejudices one would
like to be true.[4]

Confirmation bias is a fancy way of describing the
instinct to believe the worst things about people with whom
we might disagree.

One of the most egregious recent examples of this was a
bizarre story that originated during the 2016 election. Some
conservatives, already primed to not like former Secretary
of State Hillary Clinton, convinced themselves that not only
was she liberal, but part of some elaborate plot that involved
the hacked emails from her chief of staff, John Podesta.
People believed Clinton and Podesta were involved in a secret
child trafficking ring and would meet, clandestinely, at a
pizza shop in Washington, DC, named Comet Ping Pong.

Everything about this story was completely untrue, but
that didn't stop it from spreading among people who *wanted*
it to be true. So they posted death threats to the pages of
the restaurant owner, and in a frightening incident, Edgar
Maddison Welch, a young man from North Carolina, walked
into Comet Ping Pong and opened fire with an assault rifle.
Fortunately, he was a poor shot and didn't hit any customers.
He was apprehended and arrested by police.

But the damage was done to the reputation of this business owner, and the lives of those customers who survived
this shooting will be forever traumatized.

Of course confirmation bias doesn't always lead to these extreme outcomes, but it drives partisans to believe and spread information that may not be true. Welch and many others like him believed this story, despite the facts, because they *wanted* it to be true. And perhaps you reading this book or me writing this book would not likely fall for such a ridiculous conspiracy, but we are susceptible to believe news, to jump ahead of the facts, to not wait for the full story *because we want to believe the worst about the people with whom we disagree.*

Another factor that contributes to our instinct to add our voice to a chorus of critics is the way we often use social media to create a bubble or an echo chamber. Experts call this tendency a "hive mind." Groups of people come to a consensus about something without hearing or being willing to listen to alternative ideas. This doesn't just happen online. It can happen in any setting where groupthink is encouraged and rewarded. I've been in not so few board meetings and staff gatherings where it was strongly implied that any kind of disagreement or dissent, even on marginal, tertiary matters was tantamount to betrayal. This can happen on a much wider scale online. Though social media often features nasty and sometimes pointless debate, it can also encourage a kind of unthinking conformity to the reigning narrative of the tribe.

This is what people are saying. This is what the internet has decided. This is what the hive mind says we need to say. And so we join a mob without knowing it.

Perhaps nowhere was this more pronounced than in the story of a few kids who happened to be participating in the annual March for Life, held every year in the nation's capital. A video emerged that appeared to show some young Catholic kids with Make America Great Again hats picking on a Native American Vietnam veteran. The internet hive mind automatically picked up the narrative: pro-life kids dehumanizing a minority at a march supposedly in favor of the dignity of the most vulnerable human life. And people across the political spectrum expressed their outrage, including not an insignificant amount of Christian leaders, who jumped in with the chance to both condemn the high-school kids and use this as an opportunity to declare everything wrong with the pro-life movement. Powerful pundits and op-ed writers raced to declare these kids the epitome of what is wrong with America. Some even analyzed one of the kids' supposed smile as a symbol of racism and privilege.

But, it turns out, the video was out of context. There was more to the story. Much more. And twenty-four hours later, news organizations had to issue embarrassing corrections. Major celebrities and figures, who had released their armies of followers to go after the Covington, Kentucky, kids, now apologized. But imagine if everyone had simply slowed down and waited for context before declaring their opinion. If they had resisted the urge to use their platform to gather a storm against ordinary people.

Forgiveness in a Cancel Culture

There are perverse passions that tempt us to join a social media pile on, but there are also deeply meaningful reasons we react as well. Humans naturally recoil at injustice or perceived injustice. When it looks like someone is being mistreated, violated, or hurt, our instinct is to jump in and defend the innocent. This is something God has woven into his image-bearers and has made all the more alive in us if we've received the sanctifying power of the Holy Spirit. Christians are compelled by God to love our neighbors and speak up for the voiceless.

But today the news of the world doesn't just arrive the next day on our stoop in a newspaper; it is instantaneously delivered on our timelines and in news alerts. Friends and family immediately text: "Did you hear?"

And, just as we can become aware of injustice instantaneously, so it seems we can act instantaneously. In almost every other era of human history, news traveled slowly. Messengers on horseback, cables between governments, even the *tap, tap* of the telegraph. And although radio and telephone and television have been with us for a long time, still there were filters before we got our news. Anchors and reporters would sift between rumor and fact and would report what they knew. Then we'd get a fuller picture in the morning newspaper.

Today, reporting is instantaneous. A quick scroll of Twitter, where I follow quite a few local and national reporters, gives me more news than I'd get from a week's reading of the *Chicago Tribune* and *Chicago Sun Times* that arrived at the end of our driveway when I was a kid. What's more, methods of expressing ourselves have also become instantaneous. To be heard outside of one's circle of family or friends, most people who were not columnists or broadcasters had to write a halfway literate letter to the editor and hope it would get published.

Today, we can both get the news quickly and react quickly. We can thumb a few sentences and press send, immediately expressing our thoughts to thousands or perhaps millions of people around the world. This kind of power isn't just available to celebrities and politicians. Anyone can post anything on a seemingly unlimited number of platforms.

In many ways this is a welcome new reality. When a natural disaster strikes, relief and aid can be mobilized sooner. When there is a tragic death, online fundraisers can be created and money can be raised in mere hours. Missing persons can be located when millions of people spread the word. And, unlike previous generations when many voices were not part of a national conversation, the barriers to entry to speak, to write, and to mobilize are much lower. Movements can be created faster and more voices can be heard.

But the torrent of information coming at us combined with the ease of instant communication can also be damaging. And our instinct to be right, to be first, to be heard is one of the reasons we often make mistakes. Because we don't wait before speaking, we allow confirmation bias and the internet's hive mind to keep us from wisely evaluating both what we are hearing and what we are communicating. Alan

Jacobs says that our "instinct for consensus is magnified and intensified in our era because we deal daily with a wild torrent of what claims to be information but is often nonsense."[5]

We also don't realize how much of this "nonsense" is a form of entertainment, an intoxicating theater of the absurd.

Senator Ben Sasse agrees that much of what passes for news and opinion is actually a form of entertainment, "Many of our television hosts are modern-day carnival barkers. We can get dopamine, adrenaline, and oxytocin all at once. It's an adult video game."[6] Online, we operate in what David Brooks calls a "coliseum culture" where we sit around watching someone get rhetorically eaten alive. There are some mornings when I wake up and wonder to myself: *Who is the internet going to be mad at today?* What's ironic about this emerging shame culture is the way it draws out the longings of the human heart for justice and the way it tries, but fails, to mirror the story the Bible tells about righteousness and justice, forgiveness and grace.

Andrew Sullivan, an agnostic journalist, nonetheless notices that this phenomenon is "filling the void that Christianity once owned, without any of the wisdom and culture and restraint that Christianity once provided." Sullivan sees the parallel: "Like early modern Christians, they punish heresy by banishing sinners from society or coercing them to public demonstrations of shame, and provide an avenue for redemption in the form of a thorough public confession of sin."[7] Dave Zahl smartly says the online shame culture is "Christianity with all of the forgiveness sucked out."[8]

It turns out that perhaps this secular age isn't so secular after all. We have progressed, but not beyond our longings for justice. We have not abandoned our notions of sin, judgment, and wrath. There is a hell. It's called cancel culture and erasure, and we want to send the bad people on the internet there.

And yet what good news we have to offer in the real gospel. Christians possess a better story that accurately sees a world that is deeply broken, full of deep evil that must be avenged. Only we are not, as we'd like to think, on the right side of history, but on the wrong side of God. And the fire and brimstone we want to see everyone else endure is headed for our heads. This is our reality, and yet, this is our hope, for in Jesus we see God's perfect wrath exercised on a bloody cross and a lonely hill outside Jerusalem. Think of your hottest rage against the most egregious evil and multiply it exponentially. This is the anger of God against sin. But instead of directing it toward sinners, he poured it out on Jesus.

Jesus, innocent and full of truth and beauty, was the original scapegoat. Jesus was "made to be sin for us" (2 Cor. 5:21). Jesus was shamed so that our own sins might be forgiven. And God invites to his table those who were his enemies. It is sin and death and injustice, then those are cancelled, and we are invited into God's favor.

Christians should press this good news into our online conversations. We are rightly angry at evil and we rightly seek for the vulnerable to be protected and the bullies to lose their power. But any justice we seek will only ever be temporary and sometimes it's arbitrary and misguided. "We see through a glass, darkly" (1 Cor. 13:12 KJV) and often our desire to crush those we perceive to be our enemies puts us not on the side of the oppressed, but the side of the oppressor. That seemingly innocent pressing of "send," that quick post of a news story, that heated, emoji-filled rant might put us, not on the side of Jesus, but in the crowd that preferred Barabbas.

A cancel culture that seeks to isolate perceived bad guys from mainstream society through public shaming may one day come for you or your tribe. Jesus calls us to something better. Rather than erasing people with whom we disagree, he calls us to see everyone, even the person who offends our sensibilities the most, as an image-bearer of God. What gets lost in the rush to condemn is the humanity of the person we are condemning. This doesn't mean there aren't truly reprehensible people doing awful things. But it's the desire to see someone suffer, to load all of our anger and rage on them, that strips people of their humanity and makes them, for us, simply avatars to be crushed. James reminds us that in our speech we must not lose sight of the image-bearing nature of those we oppose (James 3:9).

Slow to Speak

There is a better way for Christians to read the news and process the stories that cross our timelines, which brings us back to the simple words from Scripture: "Everyone," James 1:19 urges, "should be quick to listen, slow to speak, and slow to anger."

Everyone. Every member of Christ's body. Nobody who bears the name of Christ is exempt from the Bible's command toward thoughtful speech. In the rush to speak up, in our imperfect longings for justice, we are tempted to do just the opposite: to be slow to listen, quick to speak, and quick to anger.

Being slow to speak seems bizarre in a world that is quick to speak, in a world where we can press "send" and let everyone know our opinions in a matter of minutes. But even though Scripture urges believers to, at times, speak out and to seek justice, it doesn't ever say that we have to do so immediately. In fact, the Bible seems to counsel the opposite.

In the law given to the people of God in the Old Testament, they were counseled to take time before rendering a judgment:

> "Then you shall inquire and make search and ask diligently. And behold, *if it be* true *and* certain *that* such abomination has been done among you." (Deut. 13:14 esv, emphasis mine)

And Proverbs is full of admonitions against hasty speech and forming an opinion without getting all the facts. Here are just a few:

> The one who gives an answer before he listens—this is foolishness and disgrace for him. (Prov. 18:13)

> It is a trap for anyone to dedicate something rashly and later to reconsider his vows. (Prov. 20:25)

Jesus, when unjustly put on trial, quoted from the Old Testament. He accused his accusers of violating God's law in believing rumors and hearsay in making their case against him:

> "Our law doesn't judge a man before it hears from him and knows what he's doing, does it?" (John 7:51)

This is deeply sobering to me. When I think of all those times I have posted publicly without getting the right information, when I've rendered a judgment without the facts, it is more than a digital *whoops*; it is a violation of God's law. Think about this for a moment: *We might think we are doing the right thing by speaking against injustice, but if we do this without having all the facts and spread misinformation, we are sinning.* Even if we are doing it in favor of a right cause.

God, it seems, doesn't need our fake news to accomplish his work in the world.

As hard as it is, we sometimes need to back away from our devices and pause. We must quiet those impulses that tell us we *have* to speak before we know. Whereas in the old days, we consumed news slower and curated through responsible journalists and evening news anchors, today news is instantaneous and comes in countless varieties. And many of the news organizations have contributed by prioritizing sensationalist clickbait, half-truths, and ideologically tinged news. So we should resist the urge to speak first before understanding, and we should try to fill our news diets with news sources from a variety of publications, not merely ones that scratch our ideological itches.

I'm writing this chapter in the sad aftermath of yet another horrific mass shooting in two American cities. One of the more distressing recent developments of awful moments like these is the temptation for us to go online and use the situation to score cheap political points. I see this happening, in real time, as I write this chapter and process this tragedy. The blood is not yet cleaned from the ground and partisans on both sides are using the moment to demonstrate why the other is the real enemy.

Political partisans do this, but believers should resist this with all of our might. This doesn't mean we lamely offer trite Christian phrases, but it does mean we speak thoughtfully—and probably not immediately. I'm increasingly of the opinion that platforms like Facebook and Twitter are not good forums for processing national tragedies. I'm glad, for instance, that we didn't have Twitter on September 11th.

And even when reading the news on a normal day, in non-crisis moments, we should commit to getting the whole story, rather than skimming headlines and making statements. Sometimes headline writers intentionally create titles that provoke controversy, so at the very least we should read the entire story before posting or commenting publicly. And once we get the whole story, we should still ask ourselves if we are the best people to comment. Even if a story is true, even if there is an injustice in the world or something that stirs the soul, we should each ask: *Am I the right person to comment, and is this platform the right medium?*

Ultimately, we should constantly examine our hearts with questions like: *Am I commenting on this because it makes people with whom I disagree look bad? Would I have this same position if the person in this story were in my own "tribe"? Am I willing to comment on news stories that might provoke disagreement with those who are most apt to agree with me?*

How to Read the News

So how do we process the news and interact with it online? Perhaps we begin with a commitment to read a variety of perspectives, not just those that confirm our biases. This takes intentionality because the incentives reward tribalism. If you are a conservative, you can choose a diet of news only from a conservative point of view. If you are a liberal, you can choose a diet of news from a liberal point of view.

It's a good habit to listen to people from other ideological perspectives. In other words, don't just take the news story that best confirms what you already believe about something or someone. We tend to disbelieve news because it comes from a source we might not always agree with. For instance, it's no secret that the editorial board of the *New York Times* skews very liberal, but their journalists are, for the most part, very good at what they do. I've benefited greatly from their international reporters, many of whom risk their lives to bring coverage from places around the world. I feel the same way about some of my friends who cover the news for more conservative outlets like *World Magazine*. There is a tendency among progressives to not even consider outlets like *World* or for conservatives to totally dismiss the *New York Times*, but we must recognize that there are honest people in both spaces doing very good work.

Good journalism is vital for a healthy democracy. Good journalism is often the way injustice is uncovered and the vulnerable are seen. So Christians, while practicing discernment about our media intake, should also support journalism. We are the people, after all, who should most care about the truth. We serve the One who ultimately claimed to be the truth (John 14:6).

It's also important to work to see the human side of the news. Remember that the person you are about to destroy online with a clever hashtag probably has a family who can Google their name. Do you want to be the one who caused their family pain? To knowingly spread false witness about someone by not getting the facts right says to the world that we don't value some humans like we value others. Arthur Brooks reminds us of the danger of forming opinions about people based on a single headline or tweet, saying that this practice "obscures the fullness of our human stories, eviscerating nuance and context. It is almost inevitable that when stories are reduced to just 280 characters, we jump to conclusions about others, resort to ad hominem attacks, and act as a mob against individuals."[9]

A Plea to Media

Lastly, if I may, I'd like to appeal not just to those of us who consume the news but to those who report the news. Your job, I know, is difficult in a changing industry. There is increasing competition to be quick and to be first. And there is a growing animus and distrust between the public and the media. I lament this, but I'd like to offer a perspective from someone who is often on the other side of coverage, who often hears the complaints from ordinary people who feel the media is not on their side.

In the stories I mentioned above, it was first ordinary people who took to social media to frame a narrative, but it was media outlets who added oxygen to the explosive. When a lot of ordinary people get a story wrong, it can be damaging, but when large multinational media outlets wrongly report a story, it has the potential to destroy lives and foment mob action.

We need good journalism that exposes evil and uncovers injustice, but we need media outlets willing to wait to get the whole story and to admit when they are wrong. Matt Lewis, a CNN commentator and *Daily Beast* columnist, urged this kind of transparency from media outlets in the wake of the Covington story:

> Rather than circle the wagons or pretend this didn't happen—or search for some half-hearted explanation to justify our initial reaction to the news—we should put as much emphasis on the corrections as we did on

the original story. Then, we should do some serious soul-searching about how to prevent future errors.

The first step is admitting there is a problem. We journalists, opinion leaders, and, yes, civilians must try and kick our addiction to forming quick conclusions without all of the facts.

Yes, we are living in a time and news ecosystem that compels this behavior. Competition and technological developments (I'm looking at you, Twitter) have made quick reactions, hot takes, and context-free analysis more tempting than ever. We too often would rather be first and noticed than nuanced and unread.[10]

I find myself regularly defending good journalism to conservative Christians who often feel the media is against them. Most reporters I know and read are fantastic journalists who work hard to get the story right. But there is a tendency to adopt a hive mind similar to what we described above, where reporters can subscribe to a kind of groupthink that is out of touch with ordinary Americans. It's not necessarily in the reporting, but in the framing of narratives and what stories are emphasized over and over again on cable news and in major publications and what stories are covered but assigned lower priority. Even the faintest whiff of scandal seems to dominate while stories that tell of ordinary Christians doing good work are either ignored or underreported. Our world needs more objective reporting and reporters who refuse to be activists and insist on the truth.

And it's important for all of us to admit when we've gotten it wrong. David French urges both media and consumers to be transparent this way:

> When you are found to be wrong, when snap judgments go awry, the proper response is to apologize. We're human. We make mistakes. The proper response is not to double down in digging for dirt, hoping and praying that you'll find some reason to justify your initial rage. When activists and partisans do that, they send a clear message to their opponents: They will destroy you if they can.[11]

They will destroy you if they can. Let's resist this urge. Let's follow the way of Christ. Let's slow down in our consumption, be quick to listen and slow—very slow—to anger.

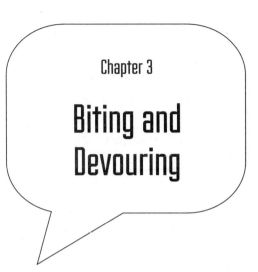

Chapter 3

Biting and Devouring

But if you bite and devour one
another, watch out, or you will
be consumed by one another.
—Galatians 5:15

knew something was wrong when I could no longer run up the basketball court. It was my first year of college at a small commuter Bible college near my home. I was still living with my parents. That morning I woke up early for my twice-a-week routine of early-morning basketball. If you are not a basketball player, you don't understand why people like me get out of bed at obscenely early times to go to the gym to bounce a round ball. But we just do. Basketball is one of the few modes of exercise that can get me out of bed early and into the gym.

But this morning started off a little weird. Feeling a sinus infection coming but too stubborn to see the doctor (a lifelong bad habit), I haphazardly grabbed someone else's leftover antibiotic from the kitchen counter where my mom kept an assortment of medicine. Grabbing random, leftover antibiotics, I would later learn, is not a good practice. But I was not yet twenty and, thus, not very wise in the ways of these things.

When I got to the gym, I started to feel a bit hot and my body began to itch slightly, but I pushed on and started playing. After only a few trips up and down the court, the itching and the heat all over my body began to increase. My face swelled up. One of my sarcastic buddies said, "You kind of look like Richard Nixon on the day he resigned." (With friends like these, who needs more friends?) They urged me to stop playing and figure out what was going on. Apparently none of us bright college students were on our way to medical school. It occurred to nobody that maybe I was having an allergic reaction.

Thankfully, I found my way to a nurse at the school who immediately assessed the situation and gave me some Benadryl. Then I sheepishly called my mother and she took me to the hospital. The nurse was right. I had just discovered another antibiotic that didn't agree with my body.

There are a lot of adjectives you could use to describe this incident: memorable, foolish, stubborn. But given how I've had to list that medication on every medical form since that day my face blew up twice its size, I would say that this was a key moment of discernment.

You Need Discernment

In her helpful book *All That's Good*, Hannah Anderson defines discernment as "developing a taste for what's good."[1] When we hear the word *discernment*, I don't know that this is the idea that comes to mind, at least for me. When I think of discernment, I think of the furrow-browed people I've met at every church I've been a part of who spend their days digging through the internet to find the dirt on prominent evangelical leaders. Or I think of the nasty people online who revel in taking down Christians with out-of-context quotes and innuendo.

But discernment—the kind Anderson encourages Christians to embrace—is far better. We live in a world filled with good and bad, beautiful and ugly, a world marbled through with love and hate, pain and joy. We need wisdom to separate what is true from what is untrue, to sort between the lovely and the repulsive, that which crushes the human soul and that which breathes life into life. Anderson writes that in order to make good decisions—about early-morning medicine or anything else—each of us needs to "become a discerning person, a person skilled in wisdom and goodness itself."[2]

Thankfully I survived my self-prescription, but you can imagine scenarios where choosing the wrong medicine or food results in more than an inconvenience and a laugh twenty years later in a book like this. I know friends whose children are deathly—and I don't use that term hyperbolically—allergic to certain foods; even a whiff could cause a dangerous anaphylactic shock. They carry around special

EpiPens in case of emergency exposure, but more importantly, they have become incredibly discerning, knowing instinctively which foods contain or are exposed to chemicals that could threaten the life of their allergic child.

The Bible encourages spiritual discernment. There is a way, for instance, to "rightly divide" the Bible (2 Tim. 2:15 KJV), meaning that there is also a way to wrongly interpret it. The proverbs speak often of the choice between two paths— not two equally good paths, but a good one and a bad one. And Jesus often used this kind of language, speaking in one instance of two gates, two kinds of leaders, and two ways to build a house (Matt. 7:13–27). The Son of God wasn't casually offering up a menu of life options, a life coach shrugging with indifference. He was saying that every human soul must choose between flourishing and floundering.

Discernment is an acknowledgment that we don't live in a perfect world, but a broken one. God's creation is shot through with both beauty and death, so it is a gift from the Creator that he teaches his image-bearers to judge the difference. That first indulgence in the garden, you might say, was a sin of poor judgment, a willful lack of discernment. The serpent seduced Eve with a kind of fuzzy naiveté, convincing her and Adam that the lines between good and evil were blurrier than what they'd heard from the Father.

And since that fateful day in Eden, the enemy has been confusing, marbling in falsehood with truth in order to lead people away from the God who created them. It is the mission of Jesus to rescue people from spiritual blindness (Matt. 13:13) and redirect their passions toward the true and the beautiful (Rom. 12:2). And it is the mission of those who have been rescued by the gospel to help rescue others by sharing with them that light has come into the world and has not been extinguished by the darkness (John 1:5).

Discernment seems to be a constant theme directed toward the people of God. Throughout the Old Testament, we can read warnings from the prophets about the importance of fleeing what is false, usually idols, and running back to the One who formed them and rescued them from peril. The book of Proverbs is essentially a constant stream of wisdom about the choice between good and evil, prudence and foolishness. And we don't just read warnings but vivid, real-life examples of discernment or lack of discernment in the characters that fill the pages of our Bibles.

The Old Testament serves, in many ways, as a kind of ongoing morality tale about what happens when the people of God pursue what seems delicious but is forbidden. You hear the lament and angst in the voices of the prophets, exasperated by Israel's lack of discernment. Here is one of Jeremiah's famous laments:

> For my people have committed a double evil:
> They have abandoned me,
> the fountain of living water,
> and dug cisterns for themselves—
> cracked cisterns that cannot hold water.
> (Jer. 2:13)

The reason God is described as being "jealous" throughout the Old Testament, the reason he weeps when his people follow after false ideologies, is because it takes them away from his care, away from what is beautiful and toward what is unsatisfying and destructive. As Moses warned an earlier generation of Jewish pilgrims, discernment is ultimately a choice between life and death (Deut. 30:15).

The warnings for God's people to choose wisely didn't stop when the prophets stopped speaking, but continue on with fervent warnings in the new covenant. Jesus, often caricatured by modern evangelicals as being a nice guy with a Che Guevara shirt who only smiles and never tells anyone they are doing wrong, nevertheless warned of coming judgment that would separate "the sheep from the goats" (Matt. 25:32). He spared no words in echoing the prophets, warning his disciples about "wolves," teachers whose words seem to be spiritual but lead to death (Matt. 7:15–20). This same Jesus is depicted, at the end of the age, as the conquering warrior, defeating his enemies (Rev. 19). So, even if you claim to only apply the so-called "red letters" of Jesus to your life, you will still end up being a person who cares deeply about truth and error, someone who . . . discerns.

To know the difference between truth and error became especially important after the resurrection and after Pentecost, as the new movement breathed out by the Spirit was spreading from Jerusalem throughout the known world. We often idolize the early church, as if this group of sanctified sinners was any less prone to heresy and foolishness than we are. Peter warned the church, saying "there *will be* false teachers" (2 Pet. 2:1–2, emphasis mine). John, the apostle of love, urged his spiritual children to "not believe every spirit, but test the spirits to see if they are from God, because many false prophets have gone out into the world" (1 John 4:1). He also revealed God's rebuke for churches that had strayed from doctrinal truth (Rev. 1). Jude said that Christians must "earnestly contend for the faith" (Jude 3 KJV).

But perhaps the apostle most serious about the damage of apostasy was the apostle Paul. Having rejected the teachings of Jesus before his own miraculous salvation encounter, Paul wrote letter after letter urging the churches of Asia Minor to reject error and embrace the truth of God's love in Christ. In his definitive letter about grace, he rebuked the Judiazers and was even unafraid to confront another apostle, Peter, over false teaching (Gal. 2:11–12).

It is in the Pastoral Epistles—1 Timothy, 2 Timothy, and Titus—where Paul is especially vocal about the need for discernment. These writings are essentially a training manual for ministry, his sagest wisdom for his pastoral protégés. Knowing his time on earth is short, Paul urges this next generation to hold fast to Christian orthodoxy. He often, in these books, uses language such as "these things" or "things you've been taught" to indicate a body of truth that comprises the orthodox Christian faith. Jude labels these core doctrines "the deposit of faith once delivered to the saints" (Jude 3, author's translation).

Paul was passionate about pastors and teachers protecting the people of God from error. Here are just a few passages where he urges discernment:[3]

As I urged you when I went to Macedonia, remain in Ephesus so that you may instruct certain people not to teach false doctrine or to pay attention to myths and endless genealogies. These promote empty speculations rather than God's plan, which operates by faith. Now the goal of our instruction is love that comes from a pure heart, a good conscience, and a sincere faith. Some have departed from these and turned aside to fruitless discussion. They want to be teachers of the law, although they don't understand what they are saying or what they are insisting on. (1 Tim. 1:3–7)

Now the Spirit explicitly says that in later times some will depart from the faith, paying attention to deceitful spirits and the teachings of demons, through the hypocrisy of liars whose consciences are seared. They forbid marriage and demand abstinence from foods that God created to be received with gratitude by those who believe and know the truth. For everything created by God is good, and nothing is to be rejected if it is received with thanksgiving, since it is sanctified by the word of God and by prayer.

If you point these things out to the brothers and sisters, you will be a good servant of

Christ Jesus, nourished by the words of the
faith and the good teaching that you have followed. (1 Tim. 4:1–6, emphasis mine)

For this reason, rebuke them sharply, so that
they may be sound in the faith and may not
pay attention to Jewish myths and the commands of people who reject the truth. (Titus
1:13–14)

People will be tempted to "reject the truth," Paul warns.
So, you see, discernment is not an optional exercise for
believers. It's necessary in order for us to see and behold
what is beautiful about Christ and to avoid the dry wells of
heresy, the death traps of bad doctrine. It's not about being
right but about embracing the truth of the One we love,
Jesus. It's especially important for those of us who teach and
preach and write about Jesus, in any capacity, to hold fast to
the faith once delivered to the saints. We will see, in the next
chapter, why it is especially important to watch our words
(James 3) and to "pay attention" to our lives and our doctrine
(1 Tim. 4:16).

Discernment versus Discernment Ministries

As much as the Bible urges us, from Genesis to Revelation,
to be people who discern, we must also heed the Bible's words
on *how* to discern.

I want to focus closely on Paul's instructions to Timothy once again. In 1 Timothy 1, Paul urges Timothy several times to "fight the good fight" (v. 18) against false doctrine. He names brothers who he says have "shipwrecked their faith" (v. 19)—not an inconsequential term for someone like Paul who experienced actual shipwreck at sea. He is concerned about some who "teach false doctrine" (v. 3) and "pay attention to myths and endless genealogies" (v. 4). Apparently in this church at Ephesus where Timothy was pastoring, some were not only caught up in false teaching but were caught up in endless speculations about numbers and genealogies, useless but interesting theological rabbit trails. By the way, their heirs seem to be doing quite well these days on the internet. But I digress.

Notice here *how* Paul urges Timothy to undergo his campaign to combat false doctrine:

> Now the goal of our instruction is love that
> comes from a pure heart, a good conscience,
> and a sincere faith. (1 Tim. 1:5)

Paul wasn't just concerned with the *content* of the teacher practicing discernment but with the *character* of the discerner. In other words, when we confront false teaching we must do the spiritual work to allow the Spirit of God to move through us so that when we engage these conflicts we do so with a pure heart, a good conscience, and a sincere faith.

In other words, discernment is not an opportunity to show off our theological brilliance or to win arguments or to own somebody rhetorically. Discernment is not about proving our rightness or the rightness of our tribe.

Paul tells the young Timothy that before he confronts someone who is in error he must confront his own soul, to ask the Spirit of God to discern his motives. There is a delicious temptation to approach doctrinal disputes, even genuine fights for the faith, with less-than-pure motives. Paul urges some personal diagnostic questions: *Do I have a pure heart? Do I have a good conscience? Do I have a sincere faith?*

Paul knew how much thought and effort were required to fight for what you believe is right. He also understood hubris and self-assurance and arrogance—that knowledge has a tendency to puff us up in arrogance. After all, Paul was a veteran polemicist, dating back to his early days as a member of the Sanhedrin, Israel's august religious body. Paul was trained by the finest Hebrew teacher in the world, Gamaliel. He'd sparred in the synagogues. He'd fired off angry arguments. And even his biblical letters, included as part of the Spirit-inspired canon of Scripture, often read as legal arguments.

So when Paul encourages Timothy to check his spirit before engaging in public exercises of discernment, he's not doing it because he's somehow soft or a squish or a sellout. He knows there is a kind of spiritual work that has to be done before you step up to the soapbox.

This is why the very next passage includes Paul's own personal testimony. He reminds Timothy that before he was a respected apostle and writer of the New Testament, he was a "blasphemer, persecutor, and an arrogant man" (v. 13).

His tendency—and ours—toward arrogance in service of the truth should motivate us toward a humble discernment. This helps us lead with both toughness and tears, boldness and brokenness. Paul knew that if he kept his own weakness in front of him, if he kept before him the liturgy of his own rescue from sin, he'd do discernment well. The truth is, we are not merely engaging theological arguments, we are speaking with actual people.

I'm afraid that today what often passes for biblical discernment fails this test of love. This is especially true among most self-proclaimed "watch bloggers" who maintain "discernment ministries." It is hard to see, beneath the contempt, the half-truths, and the cheap shots anything resembling "a pure heart, a good conscience and a sincere faith" (1 Tim. 1:5). Even in the rare case that a watch blogger isn't telling sensational half-truths and is actually exposing something alarming, the way those critiques are delivered fails the Bible's heart test.

Most of the material I've read from so-called discernment experts over the years (and I've read way, way too much) doesn't seem to come from the keyboards of people who genuinely care about those with whom they disagree.

In other words, I think there is a big difference between what often passes for "discernment" and genuine, biblical discernment. It is one thing to be genuinely heartbroken over someone who has departed the faith or is teaching something that is outside of the historic doctrines of the Christian faith; it's quite another to engage in the sin of what the Bible often refers to as "quarreling."

I think what separates biblical discernment from what we often see online is love. Love motivates us to avoid offering critiques flippantly, without getting all the facts and understanding fully the position of the person with whom we disagree.

I'm especially suspicious of people who build an entire ministry model on the practice of excavating dirt on prominent Bible teachers. When I was a kid growing up in our fundamentalist church, we were treated to a steady diet of this content, from monthly newsletters to whole publications that fundraised off of their stated desire to find controversy and expose heretics. Today, the internet has given a platform for these so-called discernment ministries to flourish. Most reflect a sinful, almost tabloid style, no different than the trash we see in a supermarket line or on a celebrity gossip website.

There is a difference between genuine discernment, born out of love, and a desire to traffic in and profit off of controversy in the body of Christ. The latter approach is, according the Bible, a sign of sin and spiritual immaturity. Paul says that "an unhealthy interest in disputes and arguments over words" and "envy, quarreling, slander, evil suspicions, and constant disagreement" is not a sign of godliness but of "a depraved mind" (1 Tim. 6:4–5). This seems extreme, and yet Paul says that someone who seeks every day to stoke the fires of controversy is not a leader worth following. In Titus 3:10 we read that these kinds of divisive people are to be "rejected." "Such a person," the Bible says, "has gone astray and is sinning" (v. 11). According to the Bible an internet troll is unfit for spiritual leadership (Titus 1:7–9).

It is time for us to call this what it is: Creating unnecessary division in the body of Christ is not just annoying, it's sinful. Listen to the words of James:

> What is the source of wars and fights among you? Don't they come from your passions that wage war within you? You desire and do not have. You murder and covet and cannot obtain. You fight and wage war. You do not have because you do not ask. You ask and don't receive because you ask with wrong motives, so that you may spend it on your pleasures. You adulterous people! (James 4:1–4)

I've become more acutely sensitive to this over the last few years as my public profile has increased and in working with a highly visible evangelical organization. Nearly every day I see the way that so-called discernment bloggers attack and vilify, not with substantial allegations of misconduct or abuse or heretical teaching, but with made-up and misleading charges, often with salacious headlines designed to get people to click. This is part of what Arthur Brooks correctly calls the "outrage industrial complex."[4]

Tim Challies, one of the pioneers of Christian blogging who has served a helpful role in helping the church discern between true and false teaching, talks about what it was like for him to be in the crosshairs of internet "watch bloggers."

I have sometimes warned about these discernment bloggers that are now all over the internet, but somewhere in the back of my mind I've reserved a place for them. I've allowed myself to believe that they may serve a helpful purpose, that even while they go too far at times, a lot of their information is helpful. I've occasionally found myself visiting some of the sites, reading their articles, and justifying it all in my mind. After all, it is important that I know the truth about Christian leaders and their ministries, isn't it?

Then they wrote about me. They wrote about my financial situation. They wrote "shocking" exposes and went rummaging through the digital trash to dig up the smoking guns. They did not just report (supposed) facts but also interpreted them. And then other blogs picked up the stories and carried them as well. And this clarified the situation for me. I wish my teacher here had been something nobler than personal attack, but sadly, and perhaps ironically, it was when I was in their crosshairs that they themselves came into sharper focus.[5]

This experience for Tim Challies could be repeated for almost every Christian leader I've ever known. It requires, in the age of the internet, a hypersensitivity and use of enormous resources just to not be the next day's headline at some Christian tabloid. It takes a toll on those who labor to serve the body of Christ.

What's sad and shameful is it's almost always self-proclaimed Christian brothers and sisters who engage in this kind of behavior. I still shake my head when I read the mean tweets or misleading blogs or libelous Facebook posts. I wonder how these followers of Jesus justify their behavior. After all, Paul says that one of the signs of spiritual maturity is to not be "quarrelsome" and to be "gentle" (1 Tim. 3:3). Ironically, some bloggers who create and spread lies about other brothers and sisters are pastors and leaders in their own churches. Yet by Paul's definition, this constant appetite for controversy, this quarrelsome nature, and the defamation of other Christians renders them unfit for leadership.[6] We should pray that they (and when necessary, we) repent. And we certainly should not continue to injure our brothers and sisters by spreading, legitimizing, or engaging this kind of content.

A Better Way to Do Discernment

So how do we do online discernment well? Here are a few questions we might ask ourselves:

Is this conflict a matter of Christian orthodoxy or a matter of foolish controversy? (2 Tim. 2:23; Titus 3:9)

There are things worth battling over—the core doctrines of the Christian faith—and there are issues that can be areas of disagreement among good friends. It's important to know the difference. And even as we disagree about secondary or tertiary issues, we can do this with both firm convictions and an open hand of love toward our brothers and sisters who think differently.

Sadly, I find too often we are slow to battle over what it is really important and quick to fight over tertiary things. Quite often those who see themselves as mature prophets might be the quarrelsome people Paul is always rebuking. We might look in the mirror and see Jeremiah or Isaiah, but in reality we are more like Sanballat and Tobiah, provoking arguments over foolish things with Nehemiah as a way of distracting from the mission of God.

Is what I'm about to publicly say, spread, or read actually true? (Phil. 4:8)

It seems so elementary to ask ourselves if something is true, but I'm surprised at how often speculation and innuendo spreads online among Christians. Every day at my job I read emails and see social media posts that assume things about the organization for which I work that are just verifiably untrue. And yet hundreds and often thousands of Christians spread untruths without taking time to do the homework of checking the facts.

Again, Tim Challies helps us discern between genuine discernment and self-proclaimed discernment ministries:

> Discernment blogs are too often marked by
> neither truth nor love. They certainly showed

very little rigor in verifying their facts about me. I do not believe the Bible mandates that outside the context of the local church a person *must* get in touch with another in order to disagree with their theology or their interpretation of facts. However, a Christian who is committed to speaking truth in love will feel at least some obligation to confirm whether details are true.[7]

Am I applying the law of love? (1 Cor. 13:7)

The love chapter in 1 Corinthians says that love "believes all things" (v. 7). This isn't naiveté or an unwillingness to hear difficult truth, but it's an unwillingness to believe and assume the worst about people. This is sorely lacking online. Just today, I read yet another headline about a friend who teaches at a conservative seminary that was made up of total lies. And in the body of the blog post was a doctored video clip, taken out of context, to make it seem as if this respected teacher, who has stood for the truth for many years, was an apostate. But if the person who shared this had simply done their homework and watched the entire teaching segment, they'd have understood what this person was saying.

To "believe all things" is to give brothers and sisters the benefit of the doubt. It means we slow down, don't jump to conclusions, and simply believe someone is faithful to the Scripture unless there is compelling evidence to the contrary. And we should even do this when a prominent Bible teacher messes up or is unclear in a book or sermon or social media post. James, in warning those who teach, acknowledges that all of us "stumble in many ways" (James 3:2). The only teacher who ever taught perfectly without any errors or mistakes was Jesus.

Love also gives us a deep humility, knowing that, at any moment, we could stray from the truth. Love helps us avoid an arrogant spirit and a posture that we are always right and everyone is always wrong. Humility recognizes, as Thomas Schreiner says well, that theological dangers don't only come from one direction. Conservatives can often rightly worry about heresy from the left, but are often blind to heresy from the right. Humility allows us not only to see the errors of our opponents but the errors that can arise from among our friends.[8]

What is my heart motive? (1 Tim. 1:5)

I think before we write that hot take on the latest Christian controversy or post about the downfall of another Christian leader or see the need to expose some heresy or corruption or abuse, we should ask the Lord to search our hearts.

We need to be honest with ourselves and with the Lord. Are we doing this because we have something to say, because we are genuinely concerned about the worldwide body of Christ? Or is there something more sinister like seizing the opportunity to be seen by the right tribe or to "take down" some ministry leader out of spite or glee.

I'm nervous, frankly, at the way we are often so quick to seize on the seeming failure or apostasy of big-name

Christians in order to get published in a prestigious publication or have our tweets go viral.

It could be that God is leading us to contribute something healthy in a way that publicly exposes or rebukes the heresy or corruption of a leader or an organization. I don't believe the conflict resolution outlined in Matthew 18 means we should *never* respond publicly to a public error. Public heresy requires public response. But we should always approach these situations carefully, as opportunities to teach and edify rather than crush and destroy. And with a few more tears.

Am I the person to speak to this at this moment?

The truth is that we don't have to engage every Christian controversy. It could be God wants us to sit this one out because we a) are not in a position to know all the facts and b) are not in a leadership position that would command the respect in taking this on.

I'm especially convicted about this when it comes to younger voices. I don't want to sound like an old man telling younger seminarians to get off my digital lawn, but I do think a bit of wisdom is important here. I'm uncomfortable with young people, with little experience and the arrogant passions of youth, "taking on" Christian leaders. I want to be careful here, because I don't want to see any important exposure of abuse or corruption silenced. But all too often, young people fresh out of (or in) their studies are eager to show the world how different they are than their parents' generation. I don't know that the motive here is love; it might rather be their own advancement.

This is why Paul encourages the young Timothy to be wise and slow when confronting someone older in the Lord (1 Tim. 5:19). And even when it comes to genuine heresy, it's often best to leave these polemics to more respected teachers. Unless, of course, you are in a position of authority in your church and need to educate those whom you serve.

I'm grateful that social media didn't exist when I was in my twenties. I can imagine I'd be the person correcting everyone that I perceived to be slightly off in their teaching. And I know my youthful arrogance was not born out of a deep desire to see people know God but out of a fleshly desire to be seen as right. The truth is that we don't have to correct every stray tweet. We don't have to "but actually" our aunt's well-meaning but slightly unclear Facebook post about her mission trip. We can actually sit out a few controversies and the world will be just fine.

Am I choosing my words carefully? (1 Pet. 3:15–16)

I'm struck by Peter's pairing of "kindness and gentleness" with "having an answer for every person" in 1 Peter 3:15–16 (author's translation). It's not just important that we be right, but that we have the right tone. This is often mocked among discernment types. Often more pugilistic folks online will point to Jesus' overthrowing of the money-changers in the temple as if a) they are exactly like Jesus and b) as if that's the only verse that talks about anger.

But over and over again, the New Testament urges God's people to cultivate gentleness. It's required of leaders in all the major qualifications in the pastoral letters, and it's sprinkled generously throughout the New Testament as one of the fruits of the Spirit's work in us.

Those who are called to deliver hard words should do it with love, gentleness, and patience. If we don't do discernment with the brokenness of heart that Paul describes, we'll not lead with love, and we'll do more damage than good. Jen Pollock Michel offers good advice: "To speak God's hard words well requires this of us: a deep, visceral compassion for the people for whom hard words are necessary. We can't revel in hard words, can't feel smugly satisfied in the task of speaking them."[9]

Are we known for love for brothers and sisters in the Lord? (John 13:35)

Jesus told his disciples that they would be known as his followers by the love they have for each other (John 13:35). In other words, as a fledgling, countercultural movement that would grow from a small band to the largest religion in the world, God's people should be known by those who look at them as people who love each other. I wonder if this could be said of the Christian movement today.

I often engage in online discussions and read conversations among believers about contentious issues and am left heartbroken over our lack of love for each other. Even if you have to express your disagreement publicly, can you do it imagining the face of a blood-bought brother or sister in Christ? When you hit "send," are you sure you have engaged that person's best arguments, or have you attacked a caricature?

As I write this today I'm lamenting a recent high-profile dustup among members of my own denomination, an argument that rose from the dirty fever swamps of the tabloid bloggers up to the most prominent news publications in America. And though I have an opinion on this particular, secondary issue, I'm saddened by the way people on both sides have chosen to debate one another publicly with character assassinations, ad hominem attacks, half-truths, and gotcha questions. Few conducted themselves with love. Most operated out of fear. And, as a result, our denomination and the larger body of Christ was not edified but sullied in the eyes of the world.

The truth is that the cross of Jesus Christ is controversial enough. It is a stone of stumbling (1 Pet. 2:8). But could it be that often it's not that ugly wooden edifice outside of Calvary that is causing so many to walk away from Jesus, but the ugliness of his followers, who rather than choosing the way of love and truth, choose meanness and discord?

So let's pursue discernment—when choosing medicine and when living the life of Christ. But let's not only commit ourselves to discernment; let's exercise discernment about the *way* we do discernment.

Chapter 4

You Shouldn't Be Teachers

Not many should become teachers,
my brothers, because you know that
we will receive a stricter judgment.
—James 3:1

There is a lot of conversation these days among pastors and leaders about platform. By "platform," I don't mean the literal stage that pastors stand on when they preach or that dirty little space where you stand when waiting to board the "L" in Chicago. When we say "platform," we mean influence. This may seem a kind of abstract conversation for only a limited number of people, but anyone in a position of authority, from parents to pastors to presidents—should think through how they are stewarding their influence.

It is important for us to think well about the shape of our public witness.

Power

Before we talk about platforms, though, we need to talk about power. When we hear the word *power*, like the word *platform*, we seem to recoil. Power can be dangerous and can often lead to exploitation and abuse of the vulnerable. There is a way of pursuing and holding on to power that is devilish. But the Bible doesn't see all power as wrong.

God granted to Adam and Eve, as part of their image-bearing capacity, a remarkable level of power. They were given authority over all creation, including naming authority over animals. To moderns in the twenty-first century, the job of naming names seems sort of passé, like our children assigning fun monikers to the family pet or their stuffed animal collection. When we name babies today, most of us either assign names that honor a family member or that sounds good to the ear.

But in the ancient world, names meant much more. They carried significant meaning. Which is why God's delegating of naming power to Adam signifies stewardship. In a similar way another Son of Adam, Joseph, would be tasked with naming the Second Adam. Joseph would be given stewardship, power, in a limited way, in order to ensure the welfare of the promised Messiah. And God would give this Jesus a "name above every name" (Phil. 2:9–11).

Humans, by our very nature, from the beginning of creation, were given power. Without power, humans could not fulfill the mandate of creation and cultivate, create, and rule. We were not made to be robots coded for automatic function.

We were made as image-bearers with agency. To possess power is to, in a small way, reflect our creative God.

This is what makes Genesis 3 so tragic. It's not that in a fallen world humans will seek power; it's that in a fallen world humans will abuse the power already granted to them by God. Just the phrase he will rule over you, whispered in sadness by God to Eve (Gen. 3:16), echoes the way men have too often used strength not to nurture women, but to exploit them.

This means that everyone, everywhere has, in some way, a measure of power. Even the most vulnerable human being, imprisoned or exploited, bereft of any social agency, has the power of their own conscience and, if they are a Christian, a connection to the divine that no brutal authoritarian can steal.

Consider Nelson Mandela, imprisoned for twenty-seven years under the cruel system of apartheid, who nevertheless summoned the spiritual strength to forgive his captors. They may have locked up his body, but they could not touch his spirit. Consider Russian dissident Aleksandr Solzhenitsyn who, while imprisoned, formed the ideals that would one day become books that would be a catalyst in tearing down the Iron Curtain. Consider even the seemingly powerless Coptic Christians, lined up in orange jumpsuits on a cold Libyan beach. These twenty-one brothers and sisters refused to denounce Jesus and went to their death, but their martyrdom has inspired a generation of God's people around the world.

Every human being, in some form, in some way, has power. It's why Paul and Silas could sing in prison, why Jesus could find "joy" in going to the cross, and why generations of enslaved black Christians could sing hymns as they felt the crack of a master's whip.

Humans have power, delegated by God. Some have more. Some have less. Some leverage theirs for the flourishing of their neighbors and the glory of God. Others exploit it for personal gain and seek what is only reserved for the ultimate source of power: God himself.

Dude, You Have a Platform

In his excellent book *Strong and Weak*, Andy Crouch shares a humorous anecdote that illustrates some of the hidden realities of leaders. He recounts a discussion with a mega-church pastor who spent several minutes of conversation reassuring Andy that in his environment, he didn't care about power. Everyone, he insisted, is equal here, and I'm not that big of a deal. This is a nice sentiment. But then Andy describes what it was like to then, after their private talk, walk into the main offices of this church with the pastor and notice everyone suddenly abandon their casual conversations and sit up a bit straighter, as if to appear to be really hard at work.

This leader did have power, power he didn't want to acknowledge. And this is the case, I think, when it comes to leaders and their platforms. I find much of the talk about power in Christian circles to be somewhat tedious and not the least bit ironic. For instance, I once listened to a wonderful podcast from a few seminary professors about the "evangelical celebrity complex," decrying platform-building. I must admit that I resonated with much of what these hosts were talking about—until I realized they both felt compelled to record a podcast about the horrors of platform and push it out to the rest of the world. I'm guessing they both hoped it would reach a wide audience with a message people outside their local circle of influence needed to hear. And if it went "viral," I'm guessing these two erstwhile platform-hating hosts would have realized they themselves had a significant . . . platform.

And this goes with tweets and blogs and magazine articles (and there are a lot) that complain about platform-building. I always wonder if people who write these things are hoping and praying they only are read by a small number of people. This is also true of our temptation to see anyone in any position of authority in our churches or homes or businesses and automatically assume they are there for nefarious reasons.

The truth is that anyone who does public ministry of any kind has a platform. Those of us who write are not writing just so our friends and family can read our stuff. We publish in magazines and journals so others can read what we have to say. After all, I am not writing this book in partnership with one of the largest Christian publishers in the world because I only want it to sell a few copies! Those who teach or preach do so knowing others will hear them and they believe God has gifted them with a message others need to hear. Those who teach Sunday school or lead small groups or teach students have a measure of public influence.

In fact, as I review my life, I'm thankful for gifted voices who had an audience big enough to reach me. I think of the pastors whose ministries aired on broadcast radio during a time when I was grappling with my faith and my calling. I'm thinking of authors like Phillip Yancey and Tim Keller and C. S. Lewis and D. A. Carson and so many others whose work has shaped my faith at critical moments. I'm thinking of local pastors who used their small church platform to burnish the truth of the gospel deep into my soul.

There is an unhealthy way to pursue power (more on that soon), but I'm grateful for those who humbly and imperfectly step into public teaching/writing/speaking roles. To lean in this way is, according to Paul, a good thing (1 Tim. 3:1).

So Christian communicators live in an interesting tension. We're compelled, by the Giver of good gifts, to pursue our callings with excellence. We're compelled to create by our Creator. And yet, we're servants of Christ. We are not to bring glory and honor to ourselves, but to our Creator. To hoard glory, to seek fame, to make our work about ourselves, not only violates why we were created in the first place, it also leaves leaders empty inside.

I wonder, for those who end up crashing and burning or for those who use their public platforms in ways that confuse or exploit, is their problem really the platform itself or the way in which they fail to see their own power and submit it to the glory of God?

Perhaps the question for us shouldn't be: How can I have a platform or should I have a platform, but what will I do with it when I have it?

We think these questions start whenever or if ever we reach the *New York Times* bestseller list or the pulpit of a 10,000-member megachurch or a regular on the conference circuit. But these soul-searching questions should happen even before you step into leadership of that women's Bible study or before you draft that Facebook post.

Influence, held loosely as a stewardship from God, can be a good thing for Christ's kingdom. However, influence stewarded poorly can be an addictive drug, an unworthy god whose adulation is undeserved. Fame can turn people into narcissistic, self-centered bullies. Power can be wielded to exploit and manipulate.

Michael Hyatt, a publishing industry veteran, shares about his own backstage glimpses of famous Christians:

> For more than thirty years, I have worked in the publishing field with Christian leaders, authors, and other creatives. During this time, I have witnessed the corrosive effects of fame. Very few have been able to handle the temptations that come with increased influence.
>
> I have seen leaders get prideful, greedy, and demanding. Sadly, it has increasingly become the norm in a world that values charisma above character.[1]

The answer for this tension is not to pretend writers and pastors and communicators don't have a platform or to shirk away influence if God allows it. I don't think it's spiritual to be sheepish or shy about the work we create with our hands. Instead, I believe, it is to ask the Lord to help us steward our creative gifts well and to hold our opportunities loosely.

If the promise of the internet, for Christian leaders, is the increased availability of getting a message out to more people, then the peril of the internet is its constant pull toward an unhealthy desire for fame. The internet promises us we can all be YouTube rock stars or Instagram influencers. We can get retweeted by famous people and think we are a big deal.

While a platform is not inherently bad, seeking fame for fame's sake can be a drug that corrupts the soul. So how do we cultivate obscurity even as we step into our callings?

Perhaps we begin by recognizing that our gifts should compel us to serve rather than be served. Jesus sets this example in John 13 by washing the feet of his disciples. Jesus didn't deny his power, but he used it in service of the disciples. A posture of servanthood keeps us from shirking away from the responsibility of our gifts and also applies those gifts toward the flourishing of others.

Your preaching, your writing, your teaching—are you viewing these opportunities not to enrich yourself or be seen, but as opportunities to take the towel and the basin and scrub away the dirt on the feet of those who engage your content? This foot-washing posture keeps us from both false humility that causes us to shirk away from our callings and from pride that seeks the spotlight at the expense of our souls.

Cultivating obscurity has to begin with intentionally embedding ourselves in a local church, a community of regular people who don't realize what a big deal we may be (or think we may be). I remember a conversation I had a few years ago with a traveling speaker whose content was so good and so edifying. I was troubled, however, by the response he gave me when I asked what church he attends. "Um, I'm not really part of a church. It's just too hard with my speaking schedule."

Speaking on behalf of Christ without being connected to the local body? What he is missing is what is necessary for his soul.

The best thing about the regular rhythms of church life is just how ordinary they are. If you polled the people in my congregation in suburban Nashville and probably every other congregation in America, very few would even recognize the Christian celebrities we think are a "big deal." And they are unaware, blissfully, of the last fifteen Christian controversies on Twitter. Being a Christian Big Deal is to not be a big deal at all.

Ultimately, we can handle whatever platform we are given by seeing ourselves as God sees us: as future kings and queens of the universe. This status is infinitely more satisfying than the cheap and faded glory we are often tempted to seek.

The Case for Careful Conversations

This conversation about platform leads us to the heart of this book. If those who write and speak and preach inevitably have platforms of various size and influence, and if this is occurring in a digital age, it would be good for us to think specifically about how Christian leaders should conduct themselves on the internet.

I'm writing this in the backwash of yet another multi-layered controversy between a few Christian leaders on an important, but secondary, Christian doctrine. And much of the controversy broke out online and among leaders in the denomination I serve, the Southern Baptist Convention. I will engage how we argue online more fully in future chapters, but here I want to specifically address the conduct of Christian leaders on social platforms.

Frankly, I've been distressed by the way some engage in manners that are both unclear and unloving. I wonder if well-known teachers or authors or pastors forget that when they tweet or post, they are in public. Social media gives us the weird feeling of being anonymous; it's so easy to speak in a fast-and-loose way that sows either division or confusion. But we are not anonymous.

The Bible has a word for this in one of the first letters written to the church, the book of James. Jesus' brother may not have had Twitter or Facebook or Instagram on his mind, but his words are exactly what we need to help us steward our influence more wisely.

James reminds those who teach the Bible—and I would include under this umbrella anyone who has a public ministry of words, from pastors to Bible teachers to Christian creatives—that this calling comes with a heavy burden:

> Not many should become teachers, my broth-
> ers, because you know that we will receive a
> stricter judgment. (James 3:1)

There is a heaviness to the responsibility of teaching the Word of God. Why is this? James answers with a lengthy discourse on the power of words. He compares the tongue with the bridle in a horse's mouth, the rudder of a ship, and fire. James uses hyperbolic language, labeling the tongue a "world of unrighteousness," a "restless evil," and a "deadly poison (James 3:6–8). So powerful is the tongue that "no man can tame it" (James 6:8). In other words, without the power of the Holy Spirit regenerating our hearts, our words can cause great damage. And even with the Spirit of God, James reminds us that redeemed sinners can either spew words of life or words of death.

We know this passage well. And yet I wonder if we've connected it back to James 3:1 and the weight of Christian calling? If not, I think we should. The reason Christian communicators are held more accountable by God is because the words we use have power. They have influence.

If the tongues (or thumbs or keyboards) of ordinary Christians are powerful forces for either good or evil, so much more for those God has called to teach and preach the Word of God.

I feel this weight when I preach. Not because I'm a big deal, but by virtue of being the leader in that moment called to open God's Word. There is an unspoken psychological effect that happens to those who hear. As we preach and teach, there is an assumption that what we are saying is from God. So when we are flippant and casual in our preaching and teaching, or if we preach false doctrine, we could lead people astray. I also believe this applies to those who create content for the church, whether books, articles, music, videos, etc. We will not get everything right, but we should try to and should clarify when we don't.

This responsibility is no less important when it comes to our social media engagement. Again, I wonder if we forget that when we are online, we are in public. It's so easy to press "send" that we often forget it is no less serious than if we were saying those things to a church auditorium or a Sunday school class. And, in some ways, social media is much more public, because the whole world can "hear" us—new believers, journalists, trolls, everyone. So Christian leaders should approach this kind of platform with a bit more caution.

This doesn't mean we shouldn't be funny or always have to be so formal or calculating, but we should recognize that when we are online, we are not in a car or a bathroom or an office; we are making statements in front of hundreds, maybe thousands of people. And our words have weight.

Ligon Duncan, president of Reformed Theological Seminary, says this about Christian leaders and social media:

> It turns out social media simply is another way of exercising our tongues, either for good or for ill. Social media amplifies the reach of our tongues. It lets our private thoughts circle the globe and brings into

public discussion conversations and statements that once would have been contained
in a small circle of friends bantering in a
coffee shop. That means it has huge potential
for evil, because we are sinners, and as James
reminds us, the tongue is hard to tame.[2]

Christian leaders need wisdom in taming our digital
tongues. People are following us, learning from us, even perhaps mimicking our discourse. This is why Paul told a young
Timothy to "set an example for the believers in speech"
(1 Tim. 4:12).

Why should Timothy set an example? Because what those
in leadership model is often embraced by those who follow.
Leaders, by their behavior, give permission structures for
those who admire them. They can unleash an army of followers to use their digital words for good or for ill, to destroy or
to give life.

Recently, The Ethics and Religious Liberty Commission
and Lifeway Christian Resources commissioned a wide-
ranging survey on American evangelicals and civility. The
researchers created what they call a "civility index." Among
the findings was this distressing data point: *evangelicals
whose political views were shaped by prominent Christian
leaders registered a very low civility score.*[3]

This is interesting when you consider that the survey
found that those who have deeply held beliefs on issues such
as abortion often scored high on the civility index. So the lack
of civility wasn't a result of believing, as most evangelicals

do, that human life begins at conception, or that marriage is between one man and one woman, but a result of watching prominent Christian leaders engage politics at the national level. In other words, many leaders have done the opposite of 1 Timothy 4:12 and have set a bad example in their speech. In doing so, they have given permission for their followers to violate what they know is a biblical imperative to speak with grace.

We've all seen this played out on social media over the last few years. Prominent pastors or teachers are carelessly articulating political opinions or engaging in doctrinal disputes in ways that disparage those with whom they disagree.

Notice James and Paul are not saying Christian leaders shouldn't speak. We should. And there are times when we need to forcefully, even prophetically, speak out against injustice or false teaching. But what we have to understand is that we are not merely being heard for what we say, but for how we speak.

In the 1990s, Charles Barkley famously said, "I'm not a role model." Of course, the whole world disagreed because Charles Barkley, whether he likes it or not, *is* a role model. And so it is with Christian leaders, especially those with massive platforms of devoted followers. You don't simply speak for yourself. You bring people with you, giving them permission to speak in the same way as you do. We should be periodically asking ourselves: *What is my online speech modeling for others?*

Sadly, our current moment doesn't incentivize this kind of responsible behavior, so we don't have many leaders who understand the weight of their leadership. As a result, in rallying their most fervent supporters, many leaders may be inflaming their worst passions. That's not to say a leader is responsible for everyone in his or her coalition, but we do have the power either to call people to our "better angels," or in the words of Rod Dreher, to "summon demons."[4]

Christians of any stature, but especially those given a measure of influence and leadership, should endeavor to set an example with our speech. People are watching us. Are we unnecessarily bringing division and rancor with our online activity, or are we fostering unity among brothers and sisters in Christ?

I'm struck by how often Paul seems to prioritize "gentleness" in every single qualification for spiritual leaders in the Pastoral Epistles (1 and 2 Timothy and Titus). Imagine if, when evaluating leaders, we actually considered their demeanor and the way they use words as a qualifying or disqualifying factor? This seems to be one of the most important character traits in the New Testament. Just read, for instance, how he instructs Titus to choose leaders. He uses three negative qualities to avoid:

> Since an overseer manages God's household, he must be blameless—*not overbearing, not quick-tempered,* not given to drunkenness, *not violent,* not pursuing dishonest gain. Rather, he must be hospitable, one who loves what is good, who is self-controlled, upright, holy and disciplined. He must hold firmly

to the trustworthy message as it has been taught, so that he can encourage others by sound doctrine and refute those who oppose it. (Titus 1:7–9 NIV, emphasis mine)

Not overbearing, not quick-tempered, not violent. Hospitable, self-control, disciplined.

In other words, those who do not regularly exhibit these traits might not be as qualified to lead as the other parts of their résumé would indicate. You can't be an internet troll and a Christian leader, according to the Bible. You just can't.

A Disciplined Approach to Social Media

Perhaps this starts with a more disciplined approach to social media. Some, like Cal Newport, have said that leaders shouldn't be on social media at all. While I respect Newport's insight, I disagree. Social media can, I believe, still be a place for good interaction with meaningful people and is still one of the primary ways of letting people know about new content and new initiatives. I also think it's an important place for pastors to learn more about their people, whether it's a sudden illness or a difficult situation at work. It can allow us a window into how to pray for them.

But we can change *how* we do social media. First, it would be wise for leaders to have someone close to advise on the timing and appropriateness of engagement on controversial issues. Pastors should be especially wise and not succumb to the temptation to forget the weight of their calling when online. Activists online like to pressure leaders to speak on every single news story and every single bad thing. You'll often see people tweet or post things like: "Why are evangelical leaders silent on _____?" As if because said leader is not as mad as that person is at that exact time on that specific medium, that he is indifferent about injustice. But leaders need to weigh their words and posts carefully. *Is this news story worth addressing and in what way should I do this?* There are moments when it's wise for you to post something, but other times you might consider that there are other, better places to express your thoughts, such as an article or in your local congregation or in some other format. And there are times when it's okay, perfectly fine, to not comment at all. Get advice. Wait. Breathe. Then decide if your engagement is necessary.

Second, imagine if we expressed more contrition when we do social media poorly. When I look back at my social media engagement over the last decade, I have to admit how impulsive and unfiltered I was, especially during election season and when big news stories dropped. In the 2016 election, especially, I lost my way. I still agree with the substance of my political views, but the way I judged others who saw things differently, the way I digitally dragged brothers and sisters in such a performative way was, now that I look back, sinful. I'm not proud of that season. At one point, a Christian leader texted me one of my tweets and said that it had hurt some brothers and sisters whom I deeply admire. This was a gut-check moment for me.

And I know other Christians have also expressed public regret. A few examples really stand out to me. Thabiti Anyabwile, pastor of Anacostia River Church in Washington, DC, an outspoken author and Christian leader, admitted:

> One of the most painful things for me over the last few years is the realization that a lack of carefulness and specificity has sometimes injured people I had no intention of injuring. That's included members and leaders in my local church, persons in other churches that are dear to me, and people I've never met and never sought to attack.[5]

Kirsten Powers, pundit and outspoken political activist, wrote of her digital engagement:

> I recently took a hiatus from social media to reflect on what role I might be playing in our increasingly toxic public square. I was not proud of what I found. . . .
>
> I cringed at many of the things I had written and said. Many I would not say or write today, sometimes because my view has changed on the issue and sometimes just because I was too much of a crusader, too judgmental and condemning.[6]

Both of these public apologies resonated deeply with me. It takes courage to publicly admit mistakes. There is no incentive for it. And yet I saw in the apologies of both Kirsten and Thabiti words that could have spoken for me. Imagine if more of us publicly admitted when we've gotten it wrong instead of digging in and defending our worst moments.

Third, Christian leaders—especially those with big platforms, would be wise to limit their own intake of social media. It might be helpful, for instance, to read few, if any, of your "mentions" or "comments" on posts. Not to be detached from the real world, but because it can give a kind of supersized image of reality. There are some who will hang on every word you tweet and think you can do no wrong. And there are some who will condemn anything you write. This is, sadly, just the nature of the internet.

I'd like to say a word about engaging that last category. There are good-faith folks online that you might engage in fruitful conversations. But Christian leaders would be wise to discern those who are engaging in good faith and those who are trolls (see previous chapter). What you may not realize is that when you engage a troll, someone whose only interest is to find controversy and disagree and nitpick, you give that person what he or she wants. And you can't ever win.

This is hard to do. I find that, like Alan Jacobs, I'm tempted often to enter what he calls "Refutation Mode."[7] The passions of the moment always drive me to want to just "crush" that troll with, you know, actual facts. But I've never seen a Christian leader engage a troll and come out looking better.

Last, it is good for leaders to build significant margin away from social media. I'm not the expert on this, but I've found that building digital-free spaces into my regular life rhythms has helped my own life and soul, as has taking extended breaks. I have found that extended time "off the grid" has reinforced to me that while digital conversations might be important, they certainly are not everything.

Perhaps the most significant lesson I've learned is how social media, especially Twitter, creates a kind of digital bubble, where the elite gather and can, in some ways, be walled off from the rest of the world. According to a recent survey, only 22 percent of Americans are on Twitter, and only 10 percent of Twitter users generate 80 percent of the content.[8] In other words, only about one of every fifty people is really spending a lot of time on this medium. So those of us who regularly do so should recognize that the opinions and the ideas we find here are not necessarily reflective of the population as a whole—or the flesh-and-blood people in our neighborhoods, workplaces, and churches.

Again, I don't think those who teach and write and influence should completely disengage. I believe social media is a way to effectively get a message across to influencers who can then spread that message to the people they lead. It can be a way of meeting and hearing new voices, of discovering new resources, and of interacting with people from around the world in a meaningful way. But, just as with any media we consume and engage, we need limits and time away, time for deep contemplation and study, time with God and away from the dull blue glow of our smartphones. The real work, as Wendy Alsup puts it, "is in our homes, in our neighborhoods, on the ground and in person."[9]

To lead, to have a platform or influence of any kind, is both a great gift and a sober responsibility. Let's pray that we steward our platforms well, recognizing we represent Christ to those who read our words.

Chapter 5

More Highly Than We Ought

*For by the grace given to me, I tell
everyone among you not to think of
himself more highly than he should think.*
—Romans 12:3

I have a weird habit when I scroll Instagram, which, lately, has become my favorite social network. I ask aloud, when viewing the images of friends and celebrities: "Who took the picture?"

Of course, I know who took the picture when it's a perfectly sunlit kitchen table, rays bouncing gently off of a study Bible, pages opened to a passage in Psalms, coffee mug cast in the background at perfect angle. The person posting this quiet-time selfie.

And I know who took the image when it's my blurry, out-of-focus snapshots of deer I met on my morning walk on the trail by my house or my son throwing a football or my daughters painting their nails. I know who is lining up that next theological tome or presidential biography so it fits in the square. It's me, trying to share with my family and friends and any others inexplicably interested in my life.

But, as I scroll, I wonder who is taking the seemingly flawless family photos, the ones with kids decked out ever so perfectly and the lighting and focus sharper than what you'd find in a *People* magazine cover shoot. I wonder how the conversations go, sometimes, when friends post "candid" shots.

> *Hey, honey, do you mind pretending like you are tossing our kids upside down? No, a little slower next time. I didn't get the full extension.*
>
> *Hey, son, can you take a picture of Mommy and me pretending to arm-wrestle?*
>
> *Hey, friend, I'm gonna look off pensively into the distance. Can you make sure you get the corn fields in the lower third of the shot?*

We said this was a book about words, and it is. But can we talk about communication on the internet without talking about the message we are sending with the images we post?

Your Instagram Life

Today a picture may not just be worth a thousand words, but thousands of dollars. A growing segment of Instagram users are becoming "Instagram influencers." Some are already famous folks with significant platforms who nevertheless monetize their reach by sponsoring various products. My blurry wildlife pics and out-of-focus vacation photos have yet to attract a sponsor, but several of my friends have mastered the art of Instagram this way, leveraging their influence to promote meaningful products and causes.

But there are others who have used Instagram to construct an almost artificial persona, a brand that sells a version of themselves in order to sell products. And perhaps the biggest demographic of would-be influencers are moms. CNN recently profiled three suburban housewives who have taken this to the next level:

> In a bathtub in Sydney, Australia, a four-month-old baby named August floats among freshly cut flowers. His mom, a radiant, sun-kissed blonde, cradles him from the other end of the tub. She immortalizes the scene with an Instagram hashtag: #momentsiwanttoremember.
>
> About 8,000 miles away, in Heber City, Utah, a mother and daughter make cupcakes in matching peach-colored dresses. The daughter, Ellie, is also wearing a tiny apron, but she won't need it. Like everything else in this aesthetically flawless #kitchen (white countertops; exotic rugs; stainless steel appliances), Ellie never gets dirty.

In Arkansas, a woman stands between her four kids on their front porch, all holding hands and dressed like they're posing for a Land's End catalog. And over in Eugene, Oregon, another mom holds her daughter to her chest under a flowering tree.

This is the world of Instagram parenting—an alternate universe where milk never spills and cherry blossoms are always in bloom. Where new moms wear a full face of makeup to soak in the tub, breastfeed, and change diapers.

It's all fake, of course—a consequence of highly-curated "influencer" culture run amok.[1]

I'm not here to judge whether or not Christians should be "Instagram influencers." As someone who has built a writing career in part by using social media to promote my writing, I don't think it's shallow to use the tools of the digital age to advance a message or promote a product. But there is something afoot, many say, about the perverse incentives Instagram and other social platforms offer for projecting a version of ourselves that is different than the reality we live.

The journalist of that piece writes about the way even those not seeking fame and fortune on the internet are influenced by the perfectly manicured Instagram life:

> If you grew up pre-social media, you may have already marveled at how different Instagram

childhoods are from the photos hanging in your childhood home. Documenting a kid's formative years isn't a casual activity for scrapbooks and baby albums anymore— now it's a daily (if not hourly) routine that takes ample time, money, and emotional bandwidth.[2]

It goes on to describe the extremes that many users will go to continue to project the good life, including hiring professional photographers to follow families around. Another article, this one in the *New York Times*, describes the new angst around honeymooning couples who feel they have to produce a perfectly "grammable" getaway. "Grammable," for the digitally illiterate, is internet code for "looks good on Instagram." The *Times* talked to one couple:

Ms. Huang Smith said she felt compelled to prove to the world that her honeymoon was as "epic" as her wedding. Before and during the trip, she researched "grammable" hotels, restaurants, and beaches. "For breakfast JP would be like, 'O.K., we're going to this place,' and I'd look at the menu before, thinking, 'What will look cute for Instagram?' And I didn't even really want to eat it! Or he'd be like, 'Let's go to this beach,' and I'd be like, 'Eh, I don't know,' because I already looked at photos and thought it didn't look pretty."[3]

Ms. Huang Smith later expressed that perhaps she should have focused less on posting pictures and more on, you know, her new marriage.

Another couple profiled by the *Times* actually moved the locale of their honeymoon from Sussex, England, to some place in Italy because of fears her friends would not think their getaway spot was epic enough. But in her zeal to have the perfectly formed Instagram trip, she booked a sixth-floor flat that had no air-conditioning!

I'm thankful I got married before the age of Instagram. Our destination was plenty "grammable," but we didn't have to argue over a hashtag, and most certainly had air-conditioning in our hotel room. But while I've not hired professional photographers to follow us around on our family vacations (I can hardly afford the vacations themselves!) and our choice of destination usually hinges on whether or not we can afford it and whether the house or hotel room fits a family of six, on a smaller level I've felt the pull of performative displays, even in our leisure. There is a weird pressure we put on ourselves when we go away of having to "report" back with stunning images of everything we do.

Tony Reinke describes this pull: "In a world dominated by the image . . . the interior life gives way to exterior show. Substance gives way to simulation."[4] In other words, we are more apt to project we are having a good time than to, you know, actually settle in and have a good time. We are a bit more motivated to show everyone our epic vacation than to actually have an epic vacation.

Or it may not be our trips we are performance-casting. It could be our religion or our family life or even our supposed authenticity. Jesus had a word for this, well before the age of pixels and posts, when he warned of the pursuit of the world at the expense of our souls (Matt. 16:26).

The Image-Crafting Life

Of course, not every Instagram influencer is projecting. There are many who use these platforms and others to build legitimate businesses, to do wonderful ministry, or to just participate in online conversation. I'm not a Luddite encouraging us to go back to some mythical golden age. The fallen pathos that motivates us to be something we are not has always been there. Only now we can see it happening in real time.

I have to tread carefully here and in this book. After all, I've made my living, essentially, because of online exposure to my work. That's how writing opportunities and book contracts and speaking engagements have come about. I owe the internet, as it were, a great deal for allowing me this life of words. Perhaps in another era I would have been discovered through my writing, which I still do frequently, in print magazines and other media. But the democratic nature of the internet has given me opportunity.

So it would be hypocritical for me to look at anyone trying to build something or make something or say something online as some kind of vice. It's not. But there is another level,

I think, beyond the normal way of pushing out one's work so others can enjoy it.

There is a difference, I think, in communicating a product or a piece of art or our work and trying to, in the wise words of my friend and pastor Dean Inserra, "be a thing." You can't quite quantify this pursuit of popularity in a spreadsheet or define it in a word, but you just kind of know it when you see it. And perhaps, in my early days on social media, other wiser people watched me and eye-rolled as I often do now about others I see who just seem to want to be noticed.

Sometimes it looks like the urge to have an opinion, a perfectly curated, pretentious-sounding opinion on things that happen to line up with the hive mind of the internet. Sometimes it looks like picking vacation spots based on how they Instagram. And sometimes it's just a kind of performative posting, a projection of a life and a persona that we wish we had.

It's wanting to be seen as the kind of person we wish we were rather than who we really are.

This is why I cannot recommend too highly Dave Zahl's book *Seculosity*, which I've already mentioned a couple of times. Zahl gets right at our desire to *be* something: "We want to feel good about ourselves, so we edit our personalities to maximize the approval of others."[5]

The subtle temptation of this kind of projection is that we often don't know we are doing it. In other words, it is easier for me to privately text a friend about another friend whom we all know is projecting and trying to perform in front of a certain tribe from whom he or she wants approval. It's quite another to see it in myself, in the way I carefully crop that photo of a book that I just *know* will make others think, *Wow, Dan is super smart!* I want people to think I'm reading this book even if I have no intention of actually reading it! And you do this as well.

I see this among fellow parents. We post photos of us doing things with our kids that we know, we just know, will hopefully plant in people's minds: *This guy is really a good dad. I mean look at his Instagram. He's at the baseball game with them. He's throwing a football with his son. He's reading a book to his girls. Wow. I want to be like Dan.*

In reality, I may have spent more time setting up said photos, with my kids begging me to put my phone down, than I did in the moment as a father, enjoying my children.

This seems especially acute among Christians, and I'm not sure why. Perhaps because we are often so defensive about our increasingly fragile standing in culture and the desire to make sure everyone knows we are so not like "those kinds of evangelicals." Or maybe there's a kind of inborn tendency in the American church toward celebrity and toward being a kind of Christian celebrity.

One of the most penetrating books I've read in the past year is the classic work *The Cross and Christian Ministry* by D. A. Carson. What's ironic is that this book was published in 1993, before the era of social media, when the internet was that weird thing nerds did in the basement. And yet Carson's critique is remarkably accurate about the lust for fame among evangelicals. Why is it, Carson asks, that we constantly parade Christian athletes, media personalities, and pop singers? Why should we think that their opinions or their experiences of grace are of any more significance than those of any other believer? When we tell outsiders about people in our church, do we instantly think of the despised and the lowly who have become Christians, or do we love to impress people with the importance of the men and women who have become Christians?[6]

What's so funny about our attempts to be "Christian famous" or to worship at the altar of those who are is that we are talking about being big fish in a really small pond. I'll never forget the time I led a youth group gathering at a small church years ago and had to educate this up-and-coming group of evangelical youth on who Billy Graham was. That's right. Church-going kids at a mainstream congregation in a Midwestern city didn't know who the greatest evangelist of the twentieth century was. And then I realized the fleeting nature of fame.

You can be Billy Graham and still there are many pockets of people who don't know your name.

So, you see, Christian fame—or really any other fame—is just so fleeting. Being a "thing" is chasing a mirage. Most of us, all of us, will labor in relative obscurity and then die, and barely be remembered.

And, as we will see, that's really okay. It's more than okay.

The Longing to Be Known

We can mock the honeymooners who shop for "grammable" locales and houses on the beach. We can scoff at those we see who are obviously trying to project a version of themselves for tribal approval. And we can sit in shame at our own attempts toward fame and approval. But we will always be frustrated until we understand what motivates attention seekers and what lies underneath our own desires to be known.

The truth is that these behaviors, enhanced by digital tools and amplified in a narcissistic age, go to the heart of genuine human longing. We were created to be known and loved, seen and heard. Woven into the ethos of our image-bearing selves is the deep-seated desire for intimacy with our Creator. Because sin has so marbled its brokenness into our human experience, we seek what we should find in God in other, less satisfying pursuits.

This is why the most famous, richest, most learned man in the ancient world, King Solomon, wrote a book about his dead-end quest for belonging. Take it from the original celebrity, the first peddler of image and influence. It's all vanity, he says (Eccles. 1:2–11 esv).

"Maybe," Dave Zahl writes, "the reason you can't stop scrolling through your social-media feed is because . . . on some level you can barely admit to yourself, you believe that if your latest post on Facebook gets enough likes, you will finally like yourself."[7]

I see this in myself. *Maybe if I write a book that reaches a bestseller list I'll finally be considered worthy. Maybe this will*

be the tweet that will go viral and lead to more opportunities.
Maybe this will be the article that will give me validation.

And here is the thing that is so toxic about our attention-seeking outside of God: those lesser idols often do give us temporary morsels of affirmation. Still, to this day, when I see my name as a byline in a magazine, I get a surge of pride. *See, you are important.* Or if I see myself quoted on social media, I tell myself, *I guess I've made it.*

This is why we are tempted to project versions of ourselves online that aren't true. This is why we are always looking for an angle to make us "Christian famous." This is why we are so desperate to find affirmation in our peer groups.

This longing is real. And the answer is not to merely shut it down. After all, the desire to be obscure can be as performative as the desire to be famous. This is why people often post multiple times on multiple mediums about the reasons they are taking digital Sabbaths, or queue up several posts announcing their departure from a particular social media platform. This is why we often have to document, on Instagram, how intentionally we are pursuing the quiet life. This can still be approval-seeking, just from a different peer group.

The answer to our fame-seeking is about more than unplugging. It's about recognizing that we are dissatisfied with the real version of who we are. We feel, deeply, the alienation from the One who made us. We know we are broken vessels, we see the mess in the mirror, we feel the weight of the fall. And yet the reality is that God has come down to us in Jesus, to both rescue us in our brokenness and join us to a new community of peers, where we are not measured by our wit or our perfectly crafted images but are approved as sons and daughters of the King.

We can bring the shame from our real selves; we can bring our brokenness over our failures; we can bring our wounded, unfulfilled souls to the place where God himself was shamed, wounded, and broken so we might be made whole again. We can step off the performative treadmill and rest in the objective reality that we know God and are known by God. It doesn't matter if ten or a hundred or a thousand people "like" us online; we are loved by the One who breathed life into us, who formed the universe, and whose assessment is the only one that ultimately matters.

I want you to read this again. Your Father loves you. You are seen and known by him. You don't have to perform like a hamster on a wheel for God to approve of you. You are enough because Christ was enough for you.

The Cruciform Life

So how do we practice this gospel reality every day in our digital lives? We begin by prioritizing our time with God and meditating on the work he wants to do in us. We need daily heart work before we engage the world.

This self-denial is not self-flagellation; it's about finding strength in our own weakness. Those things we airbrush out of our Instagram images are the very things that point us to Jesus and remind us of who exactly he came to die for. God didn't come for the person we project in our carefully manicured public images but for the broken soul we so desperately want to hide. And so we pursue obscurity, even in public, by remembering who we are and whose we are.

Again, for those of us who live in public, through our leadership of institutions and our calling to write and create in ways that must be seen and heard, the pursuit of obscurity requires a constant cross-centeredness.

We must reckon with the ever-present danger of attention-seeking and crucify it by engaging in the regular rhythm of spiritual disciplines. When I'm tempted to think I'm a big deal, I need to hunker down and get in the Word, to participate in the life of my church, to drink that cup and eat that bread, reminding myself that I'm both a sinner that cost Jesus his life and I'm now a son of the King, feasting at my Lord's table.

Second, we should view our callings as a service to others. We should always be asking ourselves how we might be using our social media activity and our public work to serve the body of Christ and to point a lost world toward Jesus. This keeps us from entitlement, from assuming too much about ourselves. Sometimes this means getting over the sheepishness that prevents us from stepping into our callings and offering our public gifts in service to others. And at other times it means stepping away into seasons of obscurity so others can rise and so we can go through the appropriate soul care.

Third, we should not hesitate to encourage others in their gifts and do what we can to open doors for them and use our platforms to point out the gifts of others. I will get into this more in the last chapter of this book, but one of the best things you can do for your soul is to make your public profile not all about you and your work. Be a digital Barnabas and launch others into flourishing.

Last, we need to just kind of lighten up and not take ourselves so seriously! The best kind of social media is when people are light-hearted and poking fun at themselves. Take the gospel seriously. Take your work seriously. But, for the good of your own soul, don't take yourself seriously. This might mean shaking up your social media posts so you're not always preaching, not always promoting, not always project-ing, but sometimes just engaging in light-hearted banter with friends. Laughter, Proverbs reminds us, is so very good for our souls (17:22). And maybe, just maybe, so is showing others our less "grammable" side—the side that Jesus sees.

Chapter 6

Act Justly, Love Mercy, Post Humbly

*Mankind, he has told each of you what
is good and what it is the LORD requires
of you: to act justly, to love faithfulness,
and to walk humbly with your God*
—Micah 6:8

I t all started at 3:21, October 15, 2017 with a tweet by a
Hollywood actress: "If you've been sexually harassed or
assaulted write 'me too' as a reply to this tweet."[1] And thus
the hashtag #MeToo went viral, as thousands of women came
forward to tell their stories of sexual harassment.

The #MeToo movement demonstrates the power of community. It gave a newfound voice to many victims of abuse
who had previously kept their stories silent for fear of reprisal or due to personal shame. While imperfect, the #MeToo
movement has exposed predatory behavior and systems that

protected the powerful in institutions such as Hollywood, media companies, multinational corporations, nonprofit organizations, and the halls of Congress. Sadly #MeToo has even revealed cover-up and abuse in the church, inspiring a spinoff hashtag: #ChurchToo.

The #MeToo movement may have happened anyway, but it is hard to imagine it in a world without platforms like Twitter. How else would the stories of ordinary survivors have been told? Would their predators, some of whom were among the most powerful men in society, have ever faced accountability?

Last year I had the opportunity to interview Rachael Denhollander, who exposed the systemic abuse of Larry Nassar, the doctor employed by the United States Gymnastics Team and Michigan State University. I'm glad Rachael and others, through the power of their voice and the #MeToo movement, have not only been heard but have led the way in helping institutions protect the vulnerable.

It is important not only for victims like Rachael and others to be heard but also for those who possess some measure of agency or platform to use their voices to speak up for the vulnerable. In my book *The Dignity Revolution*, I urged Christians to consider that the Bible's description of what it means to be human—created in the image of God—compels the people of God to stand up when human dignity is being assaulted. Jesus, in his parable of the Good Samaritan, chastised religious leaders who were looking for loopholes to love in Jesus' command to "love your neighbor as yourself" (Mark 12:31). He reminded them and us that our neighbors are often those we are tempted not to see. We find convenient excuses, on our own roads to Jericho, to pass by the poor, the lame, the enslaved, and the victimized.

For Christians, this is not an option. Though we have different callings, God compels each follower to live on mission for him in the world as citizens of his new kingdom, a kingdom that is, in the words of the prophet Isaiah, "good news to the poor" (Isa. 61:1; Luke 4:18). When we speak up for those whose voices are often silenced, when we come alongside the marginalized, we are following the example of Jesus, who in leaving his throne in heaven identified with the marginalized and the outcast. To walk alongside is to show the world a glimpse of the kingdom of God.

In other words, Christians have an opportunity to show the world by our works of mercy: "This is what Jesus is like. This is what God's new world will look like." We do this because we ourselves are vulnerable. It was God's act of mercy in Jesus to not walk by us in our distress but to rescue us from sin and death and Satan by his sacrificial death on the cross. Not only did Jesus deliver us from the evil powers; he bore the shame of our sin by accepting God's punishment—the punishment we deserved—on our behalf.

We have a rescuing, saving, merciful Savior who is calling us to go into his world to be part of his restoration and renewal, both delivering the good news of the gospel and embodying the kingdom by our lives of mercy and justice.

My friend Raleigh Sadler, who leads an organization dedicated to mobilizing the church to fight human trafficking, says it well: "God, who identifies with those most vulnerable,

commands his followers to do the same. He does so throughout the entire scope of redemptive history in his Word. . . .
Those who have truly 'gotten the point' of their religion will
naturally find themselves loving their neighbors."[2]

As the prophet Micah said to the people of God in exile,
what the Lord requires of us is "to act justly, to love mercy,
and to walk humbly with [our] God."

Heroes in Our Own Online Story

Thankfully, many Christians today are, to quote Raleigh,
"getting the point about loving our neighbors." And it seems
that opportunities to love our vulnerable neighbors have
never been more available. Social platforms give ordinary
people the power to mobilize for change with tools not available to people in any other time in human history. In an
instant we can spread awareness of some injustice to millions;
we can share powerful stories and raise money for important
social causes.

And yet it's that "walk humbly" part of God's command
that seems increasingly challenging. Just as there is a danger
of a piety that produces faith without works, there is equally
a danger of an outrage complex that produces works without
faith.

I'm writing about this right now because I know I am easily tempted toward this kind of digital heroism. My passions
for important issues can often run hot and I can be guilty
of skipping right past the "walk humbly" part of Micah. In
a social media age, with access to digital platforms so easy,

we can become part of the problem instead of part of the solution.

Stories flood our timelines about famines and fires, immigrants and the unborn, corruption and violence. We are inundated every day with a buffet of injustices, hitting us with alerts, populating our feeds, dominating our media intake. And if we are not careful, we will use our fresh awareness of injustice as a means of exalting ourselves.

This manifests in different ways. One way we do this is when we begin to treat the vulnerable not as people but as weapons in a war against those with whom we disagree. Are we really working hard on behalf of the unborn, or are we just rage-tweeting against Democrats? Are we really concerned with the children at the border, or are we exercising digital catharsis against Republicans?

I'm not just writing this to you, but to myself. I know how tempted I am by the passions of issues I deeply care about. Neighbor love is risky and hard. Advocating for the vulnerable often means we have to take positions that are not popular with one tribe or another. Because I care so much about an issue, I can easily let my passions reign in such a way that I'm not walking humbly as Micah says. I've often let my passions get the best of me and gone to battle, not with the best arguments of those who disagreed but with the caricatures of my ideological opponents. Though I'm writing a book here on how to use our words well, I'm still (as you can see by my Twitter feed) a work in progress.

If we are not careful, we can easily adopt a kind of messiah complex, always casting ourselves as the savior for those who we think need saving. We slowly begin to write a story casting ourselves as the hero—the white knight coming to the rescue. The vulnerable become mere characters in the story we are writing about ourselves.

The internet allows us to showcase our heroism publicly, to project a kind of digital righteousness before our peers.

Jesus sees right through this.

> "Two men went up to the temple to pray, one a Pharisee and the other a tax collector. The Pharisee was standing and praying like this about himself: 'God, I thank you that I'm not like other people—greedy, unrighteous, adulterers, or even like this tax collector. I fast twice a week; I give a tenth of everything I get.'
>
> "But the tax collector, standing far off, would not even raise his eyes to heaven but kept striking his chest and saying, 'God, have mercy on me, a sinner!' I tell you, this one went down to his house justified rather than the other; because everyone who exalts himself will be humbled, but the one who humbles himself will be exalted." (Luke 18:10–14)

You can imagine this Pharisee tweeting, "I'm so glad I'm not like that tax collector, who exploits the poor by skimming from the top. #stoptaxscam." But Jesus saw through his performative righteousness. The Pharisee didn't really care about the exploitation of people by this tax collector—a real issue.

Instead, he was both exalting his own identity as *not* being a greedy tax collector and projecting his goodness by boasting of his generosity.

Social media often brings out our inner Pharisee. Every day, it seems, we are at our digital temples crying loudly, for everyone to hear, that we are so very unlike those other people.

This kind of activism isn't neighbor love. It's self-love, a misguided quest for retweets and shares, the pursuit of digital approval. The truth is, we often mistake cathartic social media rants for real work.

Christians should be outraged at injustice and use their voices on behalf of the vulnerable, but we don't have the right to use them as outlets for our outrage and props for our personal identity crafting. This kind of activism is not only not what Jesus intends when he calls us to follow him into the world, it's also highly ineffective in producing actual change. Do we really care about injustice, or are we only here to cheapen ideological points?

The most effective advocates reject shame-based activism in favor of bridge-building persuasion across ideological lines. One recent example is the work of Prison Fellowship, the prison ministry founded by the late Chuck Colson. Before Colson died in 2012, he helped launch a movement among Christians to initiate badly needed reforms in the American criminal justice system. In recent years Prison Fellowship has been successful in creating a bipartisan coalition to pass sweeping changes in several states and at the federal level.

I've had the opportunity to see how their activists and advocates work to make things happen. Rather than employing shame toward politicians and religious leaders and influencers who disagree with them, Prison Fellowship works hard to listen and craft arguments designed to persuade those most inclined to disagree in language people understand. And it's been amazing to see states governed by leaders who ran on a hard, law-and-order platform change their minds and see the value in creating a justice system that better balances justice and rehabilitation, helping people and communities flourish.

I've spoken to many leaders at Prison Fellowship and often, during setbacks and times of discouragement, they resist the temptation to shame their ideological opponents, instead choosing the tools of persuasion and good communication, telling the stories of those most affected by bad policies. In my view, their work is a model. "The way to influence—and to lead," Arthur Brooks, former head of an influential conservative think tank, says, "is to begin with warmth. Warmth is the conduit of influence."[3]

From Savior to Victim

Another way we might "do justice" without "walking humbly" is through a false narrative of victimhood. I'm not talking about real stories of genuine abuse, but the temptation to latch onto a social media trend by embellishing our own story or even creating a false narrative of trauma in order to gain an audience. This is just another way of putting ourselves at the center of the story.

There are some rather extreme examples of this. Recently, NPR reported on a trend of fake crowdfunding campaigns. The stories are almost hard to believe:

- A couple who raised $400,000 for a homeless person who wasn't homeless.
- Parents who fabricated their son's cancer diagnosis and raised $3,000 for treatment.
- A man who purposely injured his dog and then raised $14,000 for emergency surgery.[4]

Perhaps the most well-known victim scam was the hoax perpetrated by actor Jussie Smollett in Chicago. Smollett claimed to have been beaten up by two young men wearing Make America Great Again hats, who put a noose around his neck and shouted racist and homophobic slurs. The media reported it and many well-known people roundly condemned the attack. But when local Chicago media began investigating, they discovered discrepancies in his story. Smollett later admitted that he set up the entire episode, hiring the boys to wear MAGA hats, put a white noose around him, and to rough him up. He was later charged with filing a false report, was billed for the cost to the Chicago Police Department, and at the time of this writing is being investigated by a special prosecutor.

Your reaction to these stories is probably the same as mine was: *What motivates someone to fake victimhood?* I doubt any of us would go to the lengths of setting up a false GoFundMe account or staging a hate crime, but the temptation toward seeking victimization is not beneath us. And in the fast-pace social media environment, where victim narratives have real currency, there is a temptation to want to cash in on the attention.

Of course, nobody quite verbalizes it that crassly. But this is what is often happening.

In our last chapter we talked about the ways we are tempted to project a more airbrushed version of ourselves in order to find affirmation from an audience. But fame-seeking and identity-crafting don't always involve Photoshop and Instagrammable waterfronts. There is also a way to seek approval by making ourselves a victim. Only this approval-seeking might be crueler, co-opting the narratives of real victims in order to exploit a movement for advantage. This is victimhood as performance art. Sympathy likes are as addictive as approval likes.

We do this, I believe, because we misunderstand the difference between genuine vulnerability and what Mike Cosper rightly labels "victimhood." Vulnerability is an act of humanity and humility, the willingness to be transparent about our real selves. But victimhood is something different:

> We have to be careful when we start talking about vulnerability, because in our culture today, there's something at work that looks like vulnerability but is actually a means of acquiring power. This is victimhood, and it's

directly related to the values of a secular age. If, as a culture, we've lost any rooted sense of morals or values, we also lose ways to navigate conflict and tension. We don't have language for it anymore because one person's definition of good is radically different from—and perhaps opposed to—someone else's. Even so, generally speaking, no one likes a bully, and it's still universally agreed that oppression is a bad thing. That fact provides leverage for cultural power; if you can claim victim status, and if you can point out the nearby bully who's oppressing you, you gain a tremendous amount of cultural power. . . . Once you gain the status of victim, you rise above any kind of moral responsibility or scrutiny. The moral imperative is about justice: How do we defend these victims from their oppressors? Any sins of the victim can and will be overlooked because, after all, they only committed them in response to their oppressors. . . . By claiming the status of victim, you don't make yourself vulnerable to risk; you're actually insulating yourself from it. You shift the conversation to the oppressor. If there's a victim, who then is the victimizer, and how can we stop them and punish them for their deeds? You also justify all manner of behavior, because, after all, you're a victim;

who can blame you for your overreactions or missteps? This dynamic creates a race to the bottom of the cultural food chain. Everyone wants to see themselves as the oppressed ones because in doing so, they will find the necessary cultural leverage to gain power. . . . Victimhood isn't risky. Rather, it's a way of shaping a cultural narrative. If we can define ourselves as victims, we can leverage the past to demonize our opponents in the present and accomplish our goals. Vulnerability, on the other hand, is about putting ourselves in harm's way. At its best, it means putting ourselves in harm's way for the sake of others.[5]

This "race to the bottom of the cultural food chain" Cosper describes seems incentivized by social media, where we can not only share our stories widely but can sit and wait for instant feedback, the inevitable attaboys and "this was so brave" responses that we crave, giving us a kind of newfound power.

Victimhood shows up in a variety of ways. It can be as simple as the kind of "Jesus loves the mess" that shapes much evangelicalism, where we compete to see who is most "authentic." Authenticity is an important virtue and necessary for pursuing Christ-likeness in community. But there is a difference in genuine vulnerability and a performative display of unrighteousness that almost celebrates sin. Sometimes we can even exaggerate our authenticity online to the extent that we are being fake about being real! The carefully staged photos of our kids being messy, the overwrought tweets about "how bad we suck at marriage," or the supposed freedom of cursing online as a sign that we are *so* not like our parents. Christians should avoid legalism and masks of self-righteousness, but performative authenticity is as bad as performative moral preening.

The Bible writers were authentic. We think of David's admissions of sin and struggle and doubt all through the psalms and Paul's humility in describing his inner battle with sin in Romans 7. But let's not forget how David embraced God's law (Ps. 119) and how Paul said that he "worked harder than [anyone]" at pursuing sanctification (1 Cor. 15:10). Of course, working on sanctification and praising God's law don't often make for nice Facebook memes.

Performative victimhood can also show up in what a friend of mine calls "identity Olympics." We should be wary of the kind of risk avoidance that Cosper accurately describes where we remove ourselves from genuine vulnerability by finding the right number of powerful identities through which we can gain access to a new kind of cultural power.

Identities shape us and help us tell our stories well. As a white man, I have much to learn from my minority brothers and sisters whose experiences are vastly different than mine. I want to lean into these conversations and be aware of the way my story biases me against a full picture of what is going on in the world. And yet, there is a way for any of us to use our status as a kind of trump card, a way of silencing others' ideas and opinions rather than engaging in helpful discourse. This kind of victimhood can be practiced across the ideological spectrum, from conservative to progressive. Conservatives can, at times, use persecution as an excuse for incivility and crassness. And progressives can embed themselves in a victim narrative in order to close their ears to those who disagree.

There is also a kind of opposition to identity politics and victimhood that makes a performance about purposely offending people with crass, needlessly offensive tweets and posts and then, when others respond with genuine offense, claiming our own version of victimhood. Political correctness is unhelpful, but responding with rudeness and shock for the sake of political incorrectness is also unhelpful. We will discuss this more in chapter 8 on civility, but a word from 1 Peter 3:15–16 is good here to remind us that while we should "give a defense to anyone" as Christians in the public square, we should also do it with "gentleness and respect." Courage and civility are not at odds, and while over-the-top speech might result in digital high fives from our tribes, it is not the way of God's people. Peter, who knew a thing or two about ill speech, urged Christians not to confuse genuine religious persecution with the natural consequences of being a jerk (that's my fresh translation from the Greek):

> If you are ridiculed for the name of Christ, you are blessed, because the Spirit of glory and of God rests on you. Let none of you suffer as a murderer, a thief, an evildoer, or a meddler. But if anyone suffers as a Christian, let him not be ashamed but let him glorify

God in having that name. For the time has come for judgment to begin with God's household, and if it begins with us, what will the outcome be for those who disobey the gospel of God? (1 Pet. 4:14–17)

Christians will, at some level, face scorn simply for following Jesus. Some will face persecution and even death. But we should never, ever confuse the consequences of our lack of civility, our rudeness, our sin for persecution. We should never use religious liberty—something worth fighting for—as an excuse to disobey Jesus' command to love our neighbors. When we make false claims to being oppressed and victimized, we only hurt the cause of the gospel.

So How Do We Walk Humbly and Do Justice Online?

So how do we obey the Bible's command to love justice in a digital age? How can we use our influence to mobilize while also avoiding a performative, Pharisaical activism?

I think we have to see social media as one of many resources in our work on behalf of the vulnerable. It's easy to mistake cathartic rage-posting online for the real work of activism. Frankly, it's often the quiet, simple behind-the-scenes work in local communities that affect the most change.

Even the #MeToo movement wasn't really birthed by an actress's tweet, but ten years earlier by a grassroots movement of activists on behalf of abuse victims. Social media gave oxygen to #MeToo, but it grew on a foundation of local work.[6]

In a similar way, I'm struck by the way so many Christians I know, many of whom are barely active online, serve the underserved with quiet acts of obedience, not looking for digital glory but serving as an outgrowth of their life with God. Around the world today, while we scroll, millions of Jesus-followers are giving their lives among the poor and the destitute. These people are not serving to be popular but because they love Jesus.

I also believe we need to do as Raleigh Sadler says: "take our messianic impulses to the cross and crucify them." We are not messiahs; Jesus is. Raleigh continues:

> As we take the way of the cross, we acknowledge that Christ is our true emancipator and that we are called to follow him as we serve hurting people for the long haul. . . . Christ not only served the poor, he allowed them to serve him as well. He could see his divine dignity in the spotted face of the leper. He could see the worth of the prostituted woman as she anointed his feet with oil. This is why he empowered the broken by allowing them to grow from a place of being passive recipients of grace to being active participants. This idea of empowerment is what is left out for many of us as we ponder Christian social action. In all of our well-intentioned rhetoric of "being a voice for the voiceless," we forget that these people already have a voice—we are

just talking so loudly that no one can hear them.[7]

Understanding our own vulnerability frees us, I believe, from our messianic, Pharisaical impulses. This is why, I believe, the prophet Micah (Micah 6:8) urges us to "walk humbly" even as we do the work of justice and James says that part of caring for "orphans and widows" is the discipline of staying "unstained from the world" (James 1:27).

To walk humbly is a posture of the heart. We can't do activism without first allowing the Holy Spirit to act in us. It is easy to get so caught up in the almost hourly pull to "speak out" online that we neglect the more important care of our souls.

Without the spiritual disciplines, we can quickly make working for God the ultimate goal of our lives rather than living with God. This is what Skye Jethani is getting at with his excellent book, *With: Reimagining the Way You Relate to God*, when he urges us to reject a life "for God" and instead embrace a life "with God": "Life for God uses him and his mission to gain a sense of direction and purpose. But life with God is different because its goal is not to *use* God; its goal *is* God. He ceases to be a device we employ or a commodity we consume. Instead God himself becomes the focus of our desire."[8]

This is why ministries like International Justice Mission take time every day to cultivate the inner life of the soul. Yes, even though there are thousands of vulnerable people needing to be rescued from traffickers, even though the demands of justice pull at them, they take time to sit before God every day, reminding these activists that the only hero in this story is Jesus, who empowers his people to move among those who have been marginalized. At IJM, all employees begin their days by spending thirty minutes at their desks in prayer before the Lord.

Prayer seems so . . . lame, so slow, so ridiculous as so many injustices scroll past our timelines. It seems weak to not tweet or post about every single thing all the time, as if by being silent you are complicit in injustice. There is a time to speak and act. Prayer is not all God calls his people to do on behalf of the vulnerable. And yet by admitting our powerlessness, we are accessing a power far greater than our words and platforms and policies.

The idea that tweeting or posting online is the only way to act against injustice is more pagan than Christian. Sometimes the best form of activism is silence and communion with God. Sometimes it's good to admit we don't know enough about an issue to comment publicly, despite what the teeming digital masses demand. Will our ill-informed Facebook rant move the needle? Will our cathartic rage-tweeting give more bread to the hungry or deliver more water to the thirsty?

We are called to bear gospel witness in a confused age, but we need the wisdom that comes from sitting at the feet of God and listening to his Spirit to know where, how, and when to act. Thoughts and prayers should never be a lazy excuse for inaction, but neither should impulsivity be a substitute for communion with God. We can join God's mission to tear down strongholds and fight injustice without tearing down fellow image-bearers.

Genuine, gospel-centered advocacy comes from an outflow of our own vulnerability in a relationship with God.

Chapter 7

Whatsoever Is True

Finally brothers and sisters, whatever is true, whatever is honorable, whatever is just, whatever is pure, whatever is lovely, whatever is commendable—if there is any moral excellence and if there is anything praiseworthy—dwell on these things.
—Philippians 4:8

Well, that's what they want you to think," a friend insisted, with particular emphasis on the *they* and *want*, after the end of a long and fruitless argument about whether or not a group of secretive bankers was plotting in smoke-filled rooms to destroy the world. I tried, in vain, to convince him that Donald Trump's election, a natural disaster in Indonesia, and the rise of the price of plastics were not, in fact, tied to a central, evil, dark conspiracy.

You, too, probably have encountered a friend or family member convinced of a conspiracy. Perhaps you've had someone plead with you to "just watch this" or have had someone tell you, convincingly, "It's been proven!" and provide the web links to back it up.

Or maybe it's not a friend prone to believing in Sasquatch, UFOs, or that the world is flat; maybe you are the one who believes these things. If so, this might get awkward because I'm pretty skeptical of conspiracy theories. But hang with me, and let's at least agree to consider why Christians should be wise about the spread of information—especially information that might be dubious in nature or seems too good (or too nefarious) to be true.

Why We Want to Believe Conspiracy Theories

Conspiracy theories might get new life in the age of the internet, but as long as there has been the possibility of conspiracy, there have been conspiracy theories. What motivates otherwise rational human beings to suspend logic and indulge in ideas that to everyone else seem rather far-fetched?

Author and commentator Tom Nichols explains this in his book *The Death of Expertise*: "Conspiracy theories are . . . a way for people to give context and meaning to events that frighten them. . . . Without a coherent explanation for why terrible things happen to innocent people, they would have to accept such occurrences as nothing more than the random cruelty either of an uncaring universe or an incomprehensible deity."[1] For many, piecing together threads to form a narrative of blame brings a measure of comfort, a place to locate our rage or find some kind of grand purpose, even if nefarious, for the brokenness of our world.

Simply put, stitching together, for instance, disparate facts about a grassy knoll, a Russian mob, and Lyndon B. Johnson made it easier for America to cope with the sudden death of their beloved President Kennedy rather than accept that a lone fanatic named Lee Harvey Oswald assassinated the president in an attempt to be famous. Theologian and cultural commentator Albert Mohler says that such ideas "fill in all the gaps of what we don't know. When we can't connect why this happened and that happened, and why this person is here and that person is doing this, a conspiracy theory helps us to tie it all together. And that's very emotionally satisfying."[2] Of course, Christians, rather than rely on flimsy facts, should instead turn to the story the Bible tells of both Satan's conspiracy to corrupt the human race and defeat God and of Jesus' divine rescue that ushers in a new kingdom conspiracy of peace and love. The gospel is more emotionally satisfying, in the long run, than a rabbit trail of half-truths.

We venture down rabbit trails because, in a fallen world, there is actually the possibility of real conspiracy. To quote Mohler again, our Christian theology tells us "someone, somewhere is always plotting evil."[3] While most conspiracy theories are debunked, there are some that prove to be true. In the Bible we see tales of high-level corruption and cover-ups. Israel's greatest king, David, conspired to commit the murder of Bathsheba's husband and was exposed by Nathan the prophet (2 Sam. 12). Jesus himself was the victim of a nefarious plot, the ultimate inside job. His treasurer and close confidant, Judas Iscariot, betrayed Jesus and worked with religious and civil authorities to bring him to trial. History is dotted with examples of high-level mischief and secret plots of evil.

But why, today, in the modern era, have conspiracy theories found new life? I think there are three factors: the weakening of our key institutions, the democratization of information, and a lack of trust in the media. First, we have to reckon with the way that institutions of power across our public life have profoundly failed us. Our political leaders have often been exposed to be dishonest and deceitful, with intricate networks of malice leading all the way to the highest offices. It's hard to pinpoint exactly when the decline in faith in American institutions began to wane, but scandals like Watergate, the sexual abuse scandals in Catholic and Protestant churches, financial meltdowns, and police misconduct have gradually eroded trust. Every institution in American society, it seems, has let us down. So, the reality of the possibility of scandal has bred in all of us the fear that everyone with power is corrupt. This is one reason we are easily duped into believing half-truths, untruths, and made-up stories.

This deficit of trust is also coming in an era where the flow of information is highly democratized. When I was a kid, news basically came in three forms: curated every morning in our three Chicago newspapers; at night from anchors with the big three news networks; and news radio stations. And if you wanted to find information about a specific person or place or thing, you'd thumb through your copy of the official *Encyclopedia Britannica* or you'd drive to the library and look through periodicals on microfilm.

Today, we seek out our own experts. We can read the first few results in Google (which probably ended up so near the top because they paid for the space), or scan articles posted by others on social media, or rely on email newsletters or podcasts. Before, the news was curated for us from the same few trusted sources; today we choose our news, based not only on ease but on ideological assumptions and biases.

This is not altogether bad. There are some real benefits to the deregulation of news. Stories that might have been ignored in a previous era because of certain biases of the mainstream media networks now get coverage. And yet the danger is that because we self-sort and find our information based on our political ideology, we can be extremely susceptible to believing what is untrue.

Senator Ben Sasse laments the corrosive impact of this self-sort on our democracy: "In the process, we've obliterated the gatekeepers who helped to ensure that information was important and reliable; we've erased the distinction between 'news' and 'opinion'; and we're losing the habits that could help us make calm, considered decisions. When it comes to consuming news, we're miles wide and an inch deep."[4]

Third, there is an impulse, especially among Christians, to distrust the media or any source of news. Too often mainstream journalists seem to have a bias against Christians in the way they cover religion or in the stories they emphasize. Too often media outlets highlight the craziest conservative, no matter how obscure, as an avatar for the whole movement while being hesitant to cover scandals that make liberals look bad. Still, we should admit that our willingness to entertain the outrageous and untrue is, in part, due to the fact that we want these stories to be true.

We not only are prone to believe the best or the worst about people about whom we want to believe the best or the worst, but we're prone to believing elaborate and often dangerous ideas that are at odds with the truth. This wanting stories to be true is what makes it so difficult to convince someone that a theory they think is so airtight is actually not at all true. Nichols explains this:

> Conspiracy theories, by contrast, are frustrating precisely because they are so intricate. Each rejoinder or contradiction only produces a more complicated theory. Conspiracy theorists manipulate all tangible evidence to fit their explanation, but worse, they will also point to the absence of evidence as even stronger confirmation. After all, what better sign of a really effective conspiracy is there than a complete lack of any trace that the conspiracy exists? Facts, the absence of facts, contradictory facts: everything is proof. Nothing can ever challenge the underlying belief.[5]

This kind of confirmation bias is why you can't argue your uncle or neighbor or Facebook sparring partner out of his ideas. It's why you can't convince a Holocaust denier or a flat-earther that they are wrong. Because in the cut-and-dried world of conspiracy, you are either with the conspirators as part of a cover-up or you are on the side of the angels who believe it.

Conspiracy theories also appeal to our vanity by giving us an exaggerated sense of being in the know, a kind of pseudo-omniscience that gives us the feeling of being in control. To know secrets is to have a knowledge that others don't possess. Carl Trueman, theologian and church historian, is right when he says that "conspiracy theories have an aesthetic appeal: they make us feel more important in the grand scheme of things than we are. If someone is going to all this trouble to con us into believing in something, then we have to be worth conning."[6]

Grand and improbable ideas not only help us find comfort but make us feel bigger when we feel small.

What Should Christians Do with Conspiracy Theories?

So maybe you've read this far and, like me, you roll your eyes at conspiracy theories. Or perhaps you are unconvinced and still think the moon landing was not in space but in a movie studio somewhere outside of Phoenix. "What's the big deal?" you might say. Does it matter if a few people indulge in far-out ideas? Who cares if our Thanksgiving meals are punctuated by wild tales of wicked deeds? Does it matter?

It does. For several reasons. First, even if speculating about the Kennedy assassination or sending an email that insists your most reviled politician is a tool of the Russian mafia seems harmless, as Christians, we should be committed to the truth. Paul urges the church at Philippi to think on "whatever is true [and] whatever is honorable" (Phil. 4:8).

Sadly, some followers of Jesus who claim to so boldly stand for truth are willing to create, spread, and post misinformation about people with whom they disagree or indulge fanatical tales about our ideological foes. Often we are the most gullible, the most willing to believe things that are not true. Perhaps this is why Paul often warned the early church against "silly myths" or fables (1 Tim. 1:4; 4:7). This is not just "going too far." Ed Stetzer, professor at Wheaton College and contributor to *Christianity Today*, says, "When you share such fake news and conspiracy theories, you are simply bearing false witness. That is a sin and it is time to repent."[7]

Christians need wisdom to discern between what is true and what is false. While we should hope that "unfruitful works of darkness" are exposed, we should avoid the rabbit trail of conspiracy theories because they both distract us from pursuing what is true and good and beautiful and because untruths damage the witness of the church. And while most crazy ideas from the internet are harmless, there are many conspiracy theories that, when spread, cause real harm. They spread misinformation, stoke fears, and can even lead to violence. As we saw in another chapter, conspiracy about Hillary Clinton and a supposed trafficking ring led a heavily armed young man to show up at a Washington, DC, pizza place.

Thankfully, he was stopped before he could commit real violence. But #pizzagate was not just harmless internet chatter. Nor is the growing movement of white nationalist ideology that is fueled by dangerous conspiracy theories that see people of color as societal problems. A young man from Plano, Texas, indulged these fantasies so much that he murdered twenty-two people in an El Paso Wal-Mart in cold blood. And the rise in Holocaust denial has often led to violence against Jewish people around the world.

These are extreme cases. But even when there is no violence involved, conspiracy theories damage reputations and hurt real people. Parents of children killed in mass shootings like Sandy Hook have had people stalk their property because they listened to conspiracy peddlers who insist their kids didn't really die but the entire tragedy was part of an elaborate "false flag" operation. Can you imagine the pain of not only losing a child to violence but also having someone track you down and harass you with wild accusations?

To indulge in these kinds of ideas is not harmless. It's corrosive to the soul, damaging for our public witness, and it hurts neighbors we are called to love. In the church, this kind of fear-mongering conspiracy causes unnecessary division.

On several occasions I've had people approach me after a speaking engagement, insisting that the organization I previously worked for was part of a left-wing conspiracy funded by George Soros. Even though the funding sources and the budget was public record, and the trustees were voted on by the members of the denomination, work every year was an open parliamentary process, still the false rumors circulate. This was mostly annoying to me at this point, but it was distressing to know that thousands were being led to believe vile things about fellow brothers and sisters in Christ.

Stetzer is right when he says, "spreading conspiracies and fake news directly violates Scripture's prohibition from bearing false witness against our neighbors. It devalues the name of Christ—whom we believe to be the very incarnation of truth—and it inflicts pain upon the people involved."[8]

We also need to examine the motivations that lead us to fall prey to such wild theories. If, as Mohler and Nichols asserted above, conspiracy theories give us a measure of comfort in troubling times, perhaps we are looking for peace where it cannot be ultimately found. Just before he urges the Philippian believers to think on what is true, Paul says that "the peace of God, which surpasses all understanding, will guard [our] hearts and minds in Christ Jesus" (Phil. 4:7). Conspiracy and intrigue gives us a sense of control, of knowing all things and being able to keep our fears in front of us. God calls us to a quiet peace, fueled by both trust in him and the mystery of faith.

Our connecting of unconnected dots is a cheap substitute for believing the ultimate story that explains the world. The Bible tells us evil and tragedy and sin find their root not in a smoke-filled room in Switzerland but with the "ruler of the power of the air, the spirit now working in the disobedient." Satan is the ultimate master conspirator and sin is the virus that has woven its way into every human heart. But we believers know that the man behind the curtain is on a leash, limited in power, and was defeated when Jesus uttered those agonizing words from a Roman cross: "It is finished" (John 19:30)!

The dots, for us, have been connected. And Jesus, the victor, has triumphed over the enemy. So while we participate with him in renewing and restoring the world, we can rejoice when evil is exposed without indulging dark and false fantasies.

The Mystery of Faith and the Seeking of Wisdom

This means we can live with mystery. Part of the reason we are so easily misled into conspiracy theories and silly myths is because we resist accepting the unknown and uncertain. And the easy reach of facts gives us the illusion of knowing all. Those quiet nights when I can't sleep, rather than rest and leave my finite thoughts to the Lord, I'm tempted to Google my problems away or find an explanation for what seems explainable. What leads us down these paths of irrational thought is both a denial of our own finite humanity and a forgetting of the humanness of others, especially those we think are caught up in some grand plot.

God doesn't want us to know everything. God's thoughts are higher and deeper and vaster than ours (Isa. 55:8–9), and this should give us comfort. He has the dots connected. He holds the worlds in his hands. He is sovereign even over the disparate strands of history and is gathering it all to himself. What great comfort.

In indulging far-out conspiracy theories, we also forget the finitude of those whom we assume are pulling the strings or plotting evil. There are some incredibly powerful world leaders and business executives and Hollywood personalities, but each of these is as human as we are. Sometimes in our fear, we assign them a power only God has. Carl Trueman reminds us, "nobody is that competent and powerful to pull them [conspiracy theories] off. Even giant bureaucracies are made up of lots of small, incompetent units fighting petty turf wars."[9]

This isn't to say we should be naive about the possibility of evil. Cover-ups and malfeasance exist. But we should resist confirmation bias and pursue wisdom. The Bible tells us that the pursuit of wisdom is priceless (Prov. 8:11). Wisdom is the antidote to the kind of raw smorgasbord of data we have at our disposal in a digital age. This means we need to have a healthy skepticism toward the intake of information.

I'm amazed, frankly, at the way we are tempted to reject the authority of those who might have expertise and grant authority instead to our favorite sources online. Because our institutions have failed us, and experts, at times, get things wrong, we often reject the hard-won wisdom of people who have spent their lives accumulating the right kind of knowledge. Nichols says, "I fear we are witnessing the death of the ideal of expertise itself, a Google-fueled, Wikipedia-based, blog-sodden collapse of any division between professionals and laypeople, students and teachers, knowers and wonderers—in other words, between those of any achievement in an area and those with none at all."[10]

Nichols's book is incredibly helpful in recognizing our need for wisdom from experts who know more than we do. Because we can Google stuff, we think we are experts and often dismiss as "elite" or "the establishment" those who have spent years pursuing actual useful knowledge in areas outside of our callings. Thinking on what is true requires us to lean on the knowledge of experts, to understand our own intellectual limitations, and to resist the lie that says we can be all-knowing.

It's actually quite arrogant for me to assume that, for example, a doctor who has studied in medical school for years knows less about my health than some random Google search. Or that my friend who works in pediatric infectious disease at a university research hospital, an elder in his church, and committed Christian brother, knows less about the validity of vaccinations for my children than I do. It's even more foolish to trust one person on the internet more than the shared knowledge of medical professionals who study these things for a living. The Bible tells us wisdom is often found, not in finding ideas that confirm our fears or appeal to what we already believe or want to be true, but in a multitude, a community of wisdom (Prov. 11:14).

And so, to guard against falling for bad ideas, conspiracy theories, or false information, we should cultivate the humility of asking, seeking, and tempering our certainties with humility. We don't know everything. We are not experts at everything. A life of faith that loves God with all of our minds requires us to seek the truth, reject what isn't true, and hold our biases loosely in order to let God transform and renew us (Rom. 12:2).

As much as we affirm that embracing truth leads to human flourishing, we have to admit that spreading falsehoods leads to human brokenness. And we should do our part to stop misinformation. This doesn't mean we have to be the annoying person on Facebook always correcting minor facts, but we should be hesitant to share or spread anything we don't know to be true and, in our circles of influence, should cultivate healthy habits of information consumption. This means self-curating what knowledge we take in by reading from diverse media outlets, not merely ones whose ideological biases conform to ours. And we should resist the pull toward conspiracy, half-truths, and tabloid-style clickbait that is harmful for a civil society.

In doing so, we may not convince our conspiracy-loving uncle at Thanksgiving, but our pursuit of truth can set an example that might push back against lies and our public witness might point people to the end of our pursuit of knowledge: Jesus, the wisdom of God.

Chapter 8

As Much as Possible

*If possible, as far as it depends on
you, live at peace with everyone.*
—Romans 12:18

You need to put the adult coloring books away and start actually reading."

This was an actual Facebook message I sent to a close friend in the fall of 2016 as we debated the presidential election. I know. It's bad. I'm cringing just reading it now, only a few years later. What an awful thing to say to a friend I love! And yet, this was where I was, caught up in an acrimonious several months of arguing, over text, on Facebook, and over the phone, over . . . politics. I'm still ashamed that this durable friendship with Eddie, that had seen us through many difficult seasons in each of our lives, was now in peril. All because of the passions of the political moment.

I don't think I was the only one who saw close friendships tested during the 2016 election. According to one survey, 40 percent of Americans blame 2016 for the damaging of a close relationship, up from over 25 percent days before the election. Given that this book is being published in the middle of another contentious, bitter contest, I don't expect those numbers are going to be any better in 2020.[1]

In the last year I've heard from many people who have said they no longer speak to a sibling or friend or parents or someone close to them because politics has so invaded their deepest relationships. I've even seen some partisans suggest this is a good thing, that politics should be the measure for our familial bonds, urging kids to shame their parents and parents to shame their kids over whom they supported in 2016.

Of course we can't blame all of this on the internet. It's easy to just say "social media" is the source of the incivility tearing our society apart. But it's more complicated than that.

And yet, this is a book about the internet, so we have to acknowledge the big part that online toxicity plays in contributing to further social alienation. Rather than bringing us together, as it promised to do, the internet has contributed to greater division along social, religious, and political lines. As Nebraska Senator Ben Sasse says, "More technology makes the world smaller, but that doesn't mean that when we're pressed together we'll hug."[2]

We're not only not hugging online, we are, in fact, often incentivized to digitally duke it out. Our social platforms, "as a consequence of their basic social architecture, reward rage, extremism, and hostility while they suffocate intelligence, charity, and gentleness."[3] There is increasing evidence that the rage that results from so many online arguments is not incidental but something that drives the profits of the very companies hosting the popular platforms. One study of social media activity detailed how media companies make money off of our outrage:

> Media executives have realized that they can drive clicks, likes, and views, and make money for themselves and their shareholders, by providing people with the most strident opinions. All this can make entertaining television and viral social media content.[4]

Christians need to be wise as to these perverse incentives. I do not think this means we should abandon these platforms altogether or even that we shouldn't have conversations about divisive topics. But we should be countercultural in the way we speak, working toward peace with our digital neighbors.

Does Civility Even Matter?

When I mention civility, I usually get more than a few eye rolls from fellow Christians. Many balk at the concept, fearing that it means a turn toward squishiness or a lack of deep conviction. I'm sympathetic to this argument as someone who has been active in the public square for many years, advocating for causes I deeply believe in. Civility should not be used as a lame excuse to ignore injustice or to shut down dissent.

The Bible warns against this, rebuking those who shout "'Peace, peace,' when there is no peace" (Jer. 6:14). Every major movement for justice has been opposed by people who wanted activists to go away quietly. Catalysts like Bonhoeffer, Wilberforce, and Martin Luther King Jr. were all met by milquetoast ministers who chose the easy path of accommodation instead of the difficult road of righteousness. So before we talk about the importance of civility, let's frame the discussion in a way that locates civility as a virtue that *accompanies* rather than *opposes* justice.

While we might be tempted to see these as opposing virtues, the Bible doesn't see it this way. I'm particularly arrested by Peter's instructions to the first-century church. At the beginning of his story with Jesus, you would not have nominated Peter to give a TED Talk on civility. After all, this is the brash fisherman whose tongue typically got ahead of his brain, who wanted to fight Jesus' enemies (even cutting off the ear of a Roman guard). He was impetuous, self-interested, and, when the pressure mounted, willing to betray even Jesus. In other words, Peter's passions were just like ours. If Twitter had existed in the first century, his old tweets would have gotten him in a lot of trouble. And yet a life with Jesus resulted in a new heart and a softening of the tribal rages that push a man away from love. By the time we get to his earnest letter to the church, Peter is urging followers of Jesus to exhibit both courage and kindness:

> But in your hearts regard Christ the Lord
> as holy, ready at any time to give a defense

to anyone who asks you for a reason for the
hope that is in you. Yet do this with gentleness and respect, keeping a clear conscience,
so that when you are accused, those who
disparage your good conduct in Christ will
be put to shame. For it is better to suffer for
doing good, if that should be God's will, than
for doing evil. (1 Pet. 3:15–17)

Peter is not urging believers to water down the central
truths of the Christian faith but to add kindness to their public witness. And let's remember that his audience is a belea-
guered, marginalized, persecuted people with little power
and agency in a Roman empire increasingly looking to punish
them for their faith in a resurrected rabbi.

What Peter is asking them to do is hard. It was hard for
first-century believers and it is hard for twenty-first-century
believers. I know that when something I hold dearly, something I strongly believe, is under assault, my blood pressure
rises and I'm ready to fight. Peter knows this emotion, perhaps more than anyone. He was the one ready to fight. But
he urges the people of God to be gentle and respectful even
as we speak truth.

It is important to understand that true civility is not a
sign of weakness but a symbol of strength. The one who is
confident in his beliefs—who knows that God has already, in
Christ, defeated sin, death, and the grave—can stand up and
fight for what he believes, knowing he doesn't have to resort
to ad hominem attacks that often mask weak arguments.

"The essence of civility is not spinelessness but self-control,"[5] says one Bible scholar, Bruce Ashford, professor, dean, and provost at Southeastern Baptist Theological Seminary.

I suspect many of us view civility as unnecessary. I've even heard some commentators go so far as to say it is a "secondary value."[6] But here Peter insists that courage and justice *require* civility. And Paul commands us in Romans 12, a passage that begins by urging first-century Christians to be so steadfast as to be willing to lay down their lives in service for the One who ultimately gave his life for us, to "if possible . . . live at peace with everyone" (Rom. 12:18). Paul, like Peter, was no shrinking violet. He was no squish. Both were martyred—put to death in the most inhumane and cruel ways by an unjust government—and yet called God's people to live out civility in every way possible. We, rage-tweeting on the internet, are not tougher or more courageous than the apostles.

In the Bible, civility is not seen as a cloak for cowardice. Civility is a primary pursuit—*as much as possible live in peace with all men* (Rom. 12:18, author's translation)—for all who call Jesus Lord.

An Appeal to a Common Humanity

You probably don't know who MaryLinda Moss is, unless you live in California or you have read *LA Times* journalist Robin Abcarian's beautifully written but harrowing account of the hostage situation that took place in a Trader Joe's near Los Angeles in the summer of 2018.[7] Moss just happened to be a customer in the store at the time a gunman, Gene Adkins, burst in and took customers and employees hostage.

I don't know how I'd react in a hostage situation. I've never had someone put a gun to my head. But I am impressed by the way MaryLinda Moss acted in this moment. Moss patiently negotiated with Adkins in ways that defused the situation. She both held off the gunman and the SWAT teams ready to deploy, potentially saving lives. What magic words helped calm Adkins? MaryLinda simply engaged the dangerous hostage taker by appealing to his humanity.

At a critical point in the standoff, Moss placed her hand on Adkins's chest and simply said to him, "You don't want to do this." Her brave actions resulted in Adkins giving up his weapon and surrendering to the police. She stood as a bridge between a disturbed Adkins and the police in a way that lowered the temperature of the situation.

Of course it would be foolish for us, untrained in hostage negotiation and criminal justice, to extrapolate from this one incident a one-size-fits-all approach for preventing future tragedy. Nor is this story a guarantee that, in the future, similarly brave victims will have the same success in preventing mass casualties. But I can't stop thinking about the way Moss simply appealed to Adkins's humanity. In treating this hostage like a man instead of a monster, she saved lives. I don't know if she is a believer, but I do know her approach borrows from the Christian concept of human dignity.

It's worth pausing and reflecting on just why Christians are called to be civil, to be gentle even in the face of slander, to speak truth wrapped in grace. We do it not as a tactic to win people over—though, as we saw in this story, it works. We are kind even when kindness doesn't pay off. Why? Because of the way God values human beings.

Consider the rich language the Bible uses to describe our humanity. Moses writes in Genesis of the beginning of humanity, and he does it with such rhetorical flourish. While he seems to rush through the creation of the natural world, the text slows to a crawl and employs great detail in describing this, the pinnacle of God's creative acts. Genesis tells us that the Creator reaches down and sculpts the first humans from the dust of the ground. And this work, unlike any of the others, came after great deliberation among the Godhead ("Let us make man in our image," Gen. 1:26). The Scriptures are telling us the forming of human bodies required a special level of precision and care. King David later implies in Psalm 139:13 that each person is knit together by God in the womb.

Theologians have wrestled with image-of-God language for centuries, and today we are still not fully sure what it means. But we do know this: Christianity assigns a dignity and worth to humans that it does not assign to any other living beings in the natural world. Christianity says there is a reflection of God in every person, even in a fallen and broken world.[8]

In fact, Scripture always presents two choices for image-bearers: we can look inward and worship ourselves and thus prioritize our well-being at the expense of others, or we can look upward toward the Creator and consider the humanity of our neighbors. The choice toward selfishness—to prioritize our desires over others—is at the root of every act of evil, from small sins to great acts of violence. It explains our incivility. James says this is why we are often so prone to conflict:

> What is the source of wars and fights among you? Don't they come from your passions that wage war within you? You desire and do not have. You murder and covet and cannot obtain. You fight and wage war. You do not have because you do not ask. You ask and don't receive because you ask with wrong motives, so that you may spend it on your pleasures. (James 4:1–3)

Jesus came to conquer those sinful passions within us and restore us to our image-bearing, God-glorifying, dignity-recognizing calling. And yet even as people who claim Jesus, we are still tempted to not see the humanity of our neighbors. Jesus is rebuking this tendency in his parable of the Good Samaritan. He says to religious leaders looking for loopholes to the Greatest Commandment, "Your neighbor is that person you are most likely to pass by on our own Jericho Roads." Our digital neighbor is that person whose political opinions we despise and whose posts trigger all kinds of raw emotions.

Imagine if we were able, like Moss, to see the basic humanity of those around us, even—and perhaps especially—those with whom we vociferously disagree? If we so choose, Christians today can lead the way in a recovery of this holistic, all-encompassing view of what it means to be human. We could start, I think, with looking across our deep divides and, instead of seeing avatars and enemies, seeing image-bearers of the Almighty.

This idea would be countercultural. According to one study, one in five Americans who identify with one of the major political parties told researchers in 2018 that members of the opposing party "lack the traits to be considered fully human."[9]

No seriously. Stop and think about this. Twenty percent of Americans don't think people of the other political party are fully human. In some ways this is horrifying, but in another way it's clarifying. That's actually what we are doing when we reduce our digital neighbors to caricatures online. That's what we are doing when we post mean things and hateful memes on the internet about our most despised politicians. James says that we are not seeing those people, those *people*, as human beings.

Perhaps this is where we begin. We look across the digital divide and see what God sees in our ideological foes: his own image and likeness.

And we can do this without sacrificing truth or a pursuit for justice. In fact, some of the most effective catalysts for change have insisted that civility and activism go together. Two examples, William Wilberforce in the nineteenth century and Martin Luther King Jr. in the twentieth century, prove that appeals to a common humanity can fuel social change.

Wilberforce constantly appealed to the humanity, not only of those who were considered less than human and bought and sold as property but of those he was trying to persuade, especially United Kingdom evangelicals. He commissioned plaques depicting slaves in chains, with the words: "Am I Not a Man and a Brother?" and the theme song of his abolitionist movement was the hymn "Amazing Grace," written by a former slave trader, John Newton. Wilberforce's gospel offered freedom to slave and slave trader alike, who find equality at the foot of the cross.

More than a century later, Martin Luther King Jr. similarly employed rhetoric of human dignity in his campaign for civil rights. There is an iconic photo of King in Memphis, surrounded by sanitation workers wearing sandwich boards that say, "I am a man." This was the crux of King's message. He was trying to persuade the white power brokers to see people of color not as problems or property but as fellow human beings. In a 1965 sermon at Ebenezer Baptist Church, King preached:

> There are no gradations in the image of God.
> Every man from a treble white to a bass black
> is significant on God's keyboard, precisely
> because every man is made in the image of
> God. One day we will learn that. We will
> know one day that God made us to live
> together as brothers and to respect the dig-
> nity and worth of every man.[10]

The basis for King's movement appealed to the humanity of his enemies in order to persuade them of the humanity of those they continued to oppress. "The nonviolent resister never lets this idea go, that there is something within human nature that can respond to goodness."[11]

This doesn't mean, of course, that movements for justice never require legal action or use of force. Terrorists should be hunted down. Laws against injustice should be enforced. And even war, the last resort, is sometimes necessary for the protection of citizens against tyrants and despots. Christians know that this world will never fully experience perfect peace until the Prince of Peace returns to restore all things.

And this doesn't mean we shouldn't ever contend, vociferously, about things that matter. We must sometimes argue, even publicly. There are necessary discussions about public policy that affects real people or debates over doctrinal truth that shapes how we see God and how we see each other. But even as we disagree, we should work to see the humanity of those with whom we have deep disagreements. This is why I agree with Arthur Brooks, who says our real problem is not actually anger, but contempt. It's not that we are too angry, it's that we are not making good use of our anger. It's not that we are mad, it's that we let our passions distort the humanity of those with whom we disagree. Contempt keeps us from seeing the personhood of our opponents.

Brooks urges us to "be on the lookout for dehumanization in everyday life. You will start to see it. For example, perhaps your favorite newspaper pundit refers to certain people as pigs. The point is to destroy your empathy for the object of his or her derision through dehumanization. Perhaps that seems like no big deal, but make no mistake: You are being manipulated to hate a fellow human being."[12]

Isn't this true? Our tribal instincts nurture the dehuman-ization of others. I think of the times my blood pressure rises and a tweet or a post or an article makes me mad. Sometimes the anger is justified, but most of our conflicts are not on this level, which is why we must again heed Paul's pleading in Romans 12:18 to, as much as possible, work for peace. There is a lot of real estate in "as much as possible," far more than we might concede. Not all of our battles are essential, not all of our fights are worthy of our energy. We should listen to Paul's instructions to fight only the "good fights" (1 Tim. 6:12).

Most of the things we get worked up about online are not good fights. Quite often it's just that we're being provoked by someone else's opinion, manipulated by algorithms and pixels to hate a fellow human being.

Community versus Tribalism

Essential to our status as image-bearers is our desire, our longing, our need for community. When God paused his creation of humans to say that it was not good for Adam to be alone, he was making a statement about the way humans were created to live with other humans in a reflection of the community experienced by the Godhead (Father, Son, and Spirit). We are relational people under a relational God. Even the emerging brain science confirms this belief, showing that our brains don't work well in isolation.[13]

Ironically, this was the promise of the digital age: to bring people together. And in some ways it has fulfilled its promise. I can text and call friends in other states and countries with little expense. I can FaceTime missionaries a continent away. And I can find encouragement and solidarity with other believers through social media.

And yet we have to acknowledge that as much as our devices and platforms can bring us together, they also seem to separate us from each other with cheap substitutes for community. What's interesting about society today is that in an increasingly interconnected world in the digital age, people seem to be lonelier than ever. We might "know" more people, but we actually do less together. We invest less in flesh-and-blood relationships than in transactional digital affiliations.

This is happening at a time when the bonds of civil society are fraying, from church attendance to local civic clubs. Many sociologists, from Robert Putnam to Charles Murray, have studied these troubling trends. One of the most incisive books I've read is the work of journalist Tim Carney in *Alienated America*. Carney studied quite a few communities and found a kind of hollowing out of civil society—as much a problem among self-proclaimed evangelicals as any other group.

People then turn to the next nearest available promise of community—their political tribe as expressed and joined and gathered online. Andrew Sullivan laments this:

> We're mistaken if we believe that the collapse of Christianity in America has led to a decline in religion. It has merely led to religious impulses being expressed by political cults. Like almost all new cultish impulses,

they see no boundary between politics and their religion.[14]

Politics often replaces the kind of community humans really need: the thick, rich, local bonds not mediated through screens and avatars. There is a difference between tribalism and genuine community.

As Christians, we are members of God's new community of believers in heaven and on earth. In 1 Peter the apostle reminds the first-century church that they are a "peculiar people" and a "chosen people," part of God's "chosen generation" and "royal priesthood" of believers (1 Pet. 2:9 KJV).

The work of the gospel is to bring alienated image-bearers into a new community of saints. "Once you were not a people, but now you are God's people" (1 Pet. 2:10). It is the work of the gospel to bring people who were estranged from their Maker into this new family.

So the tendency, the desire, the natural pull we have toward tribes or groups is woven by God into the human experience and an essential part of what it means to be a Christian. Not only are we part of the Christian community by faith, but we should also join civic institutions and groups as part of the human community. This is healthy and good for the flourishing of society; it's part of loving our neighbors, and it is essential for our witness in the world.

But there is a kind of joining that is healthy and a kind of joining that is toxic. Community goes sideways when we find our identity in our tribes primarily as a way of opposing or hating others. David Brooks, in his excellent book *The Second Mountain*, explains the difference:

> Tribalism is the dark twin of community. Community is connection based on mutual affection. Tribalism is connection based on mutual hatred. Community is based on common humanity; tribalism on a common foe. The tribal mentality is a warrior mentality based on scarcity; life is a battle for scarce resources. The ends justify the means. Politics is war. Ideas are combat. It's kill or be killed.[15]

I think Brooks is exactly right here. There is a tribe joining that is healthy community and there is a tribalism that seeks to constantly do war with everyone else. The promise of the digital age has, instead of fostering community, led to much isolation that masks itself as community, depriving us of the healthy connection we were created for. And were we honest, we've all been tempted to practice this. We may be making voting decisions, church decisions, and even friendship decisions not because of shared interests but shared enemies.

Community invites, learns from others, and helps us grow. Tribalism excludes, and it elevates secondary identities above primary missions. At its worst, tribalism leads to radicalization, the dangerous and growing epidemic that is increasingly leading to violence as young men are catechized into fake warfare by a foray into the evil portals of the internet. I fear this epidemic of radicalization of young men is going to be as serious an issue for the church as the issue of pornography.

But even in seemingly harmless ways, tribalism keeps us, ultimately, from the mission of God, sorting us artificially into increasingly narrow tribes that do battle with each other rather than join hands to share the gospel and love our neighbors. Dave Zahl is right when he says, "Whatever your conviction or interest, no matter how fringe or toxic, a community exists online that will reinforce it. A few clicks are all it takes to find allies who will confirm the righteousness of your opinions, as well as common enemies to fortify your tribe. It's intoxicating, radicalizing."[16]

It's intoxicating. It's radicalizing. And yet, it's corrosive to genuine Christian faith and unity. We were, after all, baptized into the body of Christ as a peculiar people, not as a way of elevating our own self-righteousness but as a way of being in the world as a light to those who seek the truth.

The Church: The Antidote for Tribalism

This is why I believe the ancient and analog rhythms of church life are, ironically, the solution for our increasing isolation in a digital age. Church life, done right, helps us cultivate local community, offline, with real people who are different than us. The internet can help *foster* real-world community by connecting us, making communication easier, etc. But it cannot *replace* embodied, flesh-and-blood interactions.

I believe incivility is a real, dangerous societal issue. Just listen to a warning by former NATO Supreme Allied

Commander, General James Mattis, former United States Defense Secretary:

> What concerns me most as a military man is not our external adversaries; it is our internal divisiveness. We are dividing into hostile tribes cheering against each other, fueled by emotion and a mutual disdain that jeopardizes our future, instead of rediscovering our common ground and finding solutions.
>
> All Americans need to recognize that our democracy is an experiment—and one that can be reversed. We all know that we're better than our current politics. Tribalism must not be allowed to destroy our experiment.[17]

Think about this. One of the most decorated generals in American history, who was once charged with safeguarding America and her allies, sees civility as a serious threat to American democracy. So if General Mattis sees incivility is a societal problem, shouldn't we? God's people need to take this issue seriously. Incivility is affecting the flourishing of our neighbors and the witness of the church.

So what can we do?

First, we can begin by repenting of our own acts of incivility and our own unwillingness to listen and learn from those who are different. The gospel demands we get out of our ghettos and into the world. We come together on Sunday in solidarity with each other and with Christ but then are called to go into the world for the sake of his name. We can't do that if we are absent from the important civic life of our communities and if we filter our news intake from sources that only confirm our worldview.

Second, we need to adopt what Trevin Wax calls "a posture of reasonableness" toward those who disagree with us. This, Wax writes, "radiates outward in a world darkened by constant cycles of outrage."[18] We've seen how Christian discipleship should be moving us toward a practice of gentleness. This doesn't mean squishy disagreement; it means that we consider that perhaps the person on the other side of a political disagreement is not a monster, but a human being, created in the image of God. If you are progressive-leaning, you need to stop seeing conservatives as the enemy. If you are conservative-leaning, you need to stop seeing progressives as the enemy. Everyone on the right is not a racist and everyone on the left is not a Marxist. In fact, dismissing their humanity, putting people in groups, is a sign of insecurity in our own positions.

Signs of Hope

Even as many warn of the dangers of our increasing incivility and as the witness of the church has often been compromised by our lack of public grace, there are signs of hope.

One recent survey[19] shows that evangelicals who believe in the fundamentals of the gospel story, the death and resurrection of Jesus Christ as the atoning sacrifice for sin, scored higher levels of civility. And those who believed in what the Bible says about human dignity also scored higher levels of civility. And this should not surprise us, because kindness, even in the face of deep disagreement, is a core virtue, a fruit of the Spirit's work in us (Gal. 5:16). In other words, while there are many and varied causes of our social fracture, Christians have the resources, at the heart of our faith, to embody what civility looks like.

We can also find slivers of hope in the ways it seems some are trying to work for unity. Not long ago, after yet another mass shooting, two prominent people on opposite sides of a contentious national issue—gun rights—came together to meet and discuss ways to work together. Alyssa Milano, an actress known for her vocally progressive views on gun rights, tweeted a challenge to Senator Ted Cruz, someone known for his vocally conservative views on gun rights. After a few sharp back-and-forth exchanges, the two publicly agreed to meet. They did, and afterward, both expressed how good it was to sit down and find common ground—even as they acknowledged they'd likely never fully agree with one another.

This is a small example in a world seemingly awash in strife, but it's a good example nonetheless. Not an earth-shattering development, but a small sign of civil progress. But it will take many more things like this, big and small, in local communities and around the country. I'm heartened by groups like Better Angels, which brings together Republicans and Democrats from across the country in local chapters to encourage conversations around shared ideals and working together toward common solutions.

And we Christians can and should take the lead in these moments. But it will take enormous courage, because tribal sorting and digital algorithms incentivize us the other way. People who thrive off of controversy are looking for signs of weakness, especially in Christian leaders. But it is Jesus who tells us we can both hold fast to truth and also embody grace. Those of us with influence should use our platforms to show the world what this looks like, refusing and resisting the urge toward tribalism and contempt.

By the way, remember my friend Eddie whom I mentioned at the beginning of this chapter? We did nearly lose our friendship over a debate about politics. How stupid, right? Well, after two months, we reconciled. I can't remember if he called me or if I called him, but both of us apologized (though I did way more sinning than he). I told him I was sorry I let the passions of the political moment nearly destroy a lifelong friendship. He accepted, and we talk or text nearly every week.

I've had to do this with other friends, both online and offline. It's not too late to apologize, to send someone a note, to pick up the phone, to write a letter seeking to restore what has been lost. It's not too late to repent of our uncivil ways.

Chapter 9

An Analog Church in a Digital Age

. . . not neglecting to gather together,
as some are in the habit of doing, but
encouraging each other, and all the
more as you see the day approaching.
—Hebrews 10:25

y wife and I were substitute teaching a fifth-grade Sunday school class at church a few years ago when a precocious boy came in late and offered, "I'm so sorry, Mr. Darling. I'm not gonna be any use today, my iPhone isn't charged."

I didn't know whether to laugh or cry. But this kid, like most other kids in this generation, has grown up in a world where the Bible is not merely a book with pages but an app on a device. I reassured him by handing him a spare copy of God's Word and letting him know this paperback copy would not run out of power (pun so deliciously intended!). I also encouraged him, as I encourage (read: *demand*) my own kids, to bring a physical copy of the Bible to church.

I think of this this story often as I reflect on the ways church life converges and conflicts with our digital age. In an era of loneliness and spectacle, how can our life together in Christ heal fragile souls and point people toward the slower rhythms of worship and biblical life?

This Analog Life

When I pastored my first church, I stepped into an older congregation with a worship style set in the 1980s. The members were faithful, godly, and eager for revitalization. So I plunged in as an eager, slightly cocksure, thirty-year-old pastor who had not been to seminary. My first few moves were aimed at what I considered small, noncontroversial issues, the first of which was to project our music on the wall rather than a screen. The previous pastor had made the bold move to install the projector and screen that, when raised or lowered, made a cringe-inducing noise that greeted me every time I got up to preach, forcing me to plead even more passionately to the Lord for unction on my way from the chair to the pulpit. I naively thought that simply restoring what I considered a common-sense practice would be received warmly by everyone in the church.

I was wrong. Most folks were either nonplussed or welcomed the return to late 1990's technology. But there was one couple with the "gift of discernment," or so they assured me several times. Given that this was an anchor family in a small congregation that could ill-afford to lose a critical mass of members, I patiently listened to their concerns and tried to mollify them with practical and biblical justifications. But I was unsuccessful, and this couple took their talents down the street.

It's been over a decade since that worship skirmish, and I still think about those conversations, though today I'm a bit more wistful and slightly more sympathetic to what I considered then to be a ridiculous concern about worship. I still think we made the right move to project song lyrics on the wall and to change our worship style. And yet I wonder if perhaps a bit more of that cautious skepticism is more warranted in this digital age.

This doesn't mean Christians should be afraid of innovation. On the contrary, technology is, at its simplest, an act of creation. As God's image-bearers, humans are compelled to create by a Creator who has uniquely gifted us with both the ability and the mandate to take raw materials and build beautiful things. In fact, we often think of devices and screens when we use the word "technology," but, every new innovation is technology. At some point the wheel, alloyed steel, and printable type were radical new technologies. Faithful Christian living is not synonymous with backwardness. After all, at the end of the age, Christ will return to usher in the New Jerusalem as a city, not a garden. We are the people who look forward.

So in our worship spaces it is right and good to use modern conveniences to improve a worship experience. We shouldn't always default to a curmudgeonly posture. I'm glad, as I'm sure you are, that in church on Sunday we will have air-conditioning or heat, electric lights, and comfortable pews. These things aren't necessary to worship God, but their absence does not bring us any closer to him either. And at one time, the things we assume have been part of the long tradition of church life, like pews, pulpits, and hymnals, were modern and controversial.[1] So we should all approach the intersection of worship and technology with a bit more humility and openhandedness. Regardless of what style we might prefer, even the most conservative approach is contextualized to a specific era and specific culture. Even the churches claiming a "New Testament" model are conducting services that would mystify to the first Christians.

And yet while we hold our models and preferences loosely, we should still carry at least a hint of that elderly couple's sensibility in our minds when we think about what's next and what's new. No, we shouldn't be cranky about worship just because we don't like it and haven't heard it or don't understand it. We might, however, insist that we approach church with a sense of awe and symbols of the sacred when we gather on Sunday, whether we are meeting in a cathedral or a classroom. While technology can be a good act of cultivating God's good earth, it can also be, in a fallen world, a disorienting distraction away from the pursuit of communion with God.

In other words, there is something distinct about what we do on Sundays. It's not just another show, another piece of content, another screen to engage. The gathering of God's people is a divinely orchestrated event, empowered by God's Spirit, an act of warfare upon the idols of the age. It's also rest for weary souls, seared by digital exhaustion. The physical gathering of God's people on Sunday might be the very antidote for a world fragmented into tribes, sorted by algorithms into narrow subcategories and engaging in quasi-relationships mediated by microchips and glass. This is why we shouldn't race too quickly to make the church experience like every other experience during the week, why we should proceed cautiously with the assimilation of screens and pixels into our weekly liturgy. Our weekly gatherings shouldn't be one more burden for the digitally exhausted but should serve as a place of soul rest, a rebuke of sorts to the digital gods.

This is especially important, I think, for the generation that likely most wants church to be like their iPhones. In her book, *iGen*, Jean Twenge describes Generation Z, the first fully wired cohort in human history. This is going to make me sound, at forty-two years of age, like an old man, but do indulge me for a moment. I'm a member of Generation X. Along with most millennials, we were introduced to the smartphone as teens or adults. But our kids never knew a time when there weren't smartphones, high-speed internet, social media, and streaming video. Twenge synthesizes the data and finds some surprising and alarming pathologies among Generation Z. There is good news: drunk driving, illicit sex, and homicides are way down. But there is some disturbing news: loneliness, depression, and suicide are at frighteningly high levels. And even among those who aren't at risk, there is a worrisome drop in social gathering and an alarming stunting of social skills. It turns out, Twenge explains, that socializing with friends and family is essential for brain development, that "in-person social interaction is much better for mental health than electronic communication."[2]

So what many people in this age increasingly are longing for, though may not articulate, is rest, a kind of spiritual Sabbath from their devices. And the church can offer them good news. There is refuge in the analog rhythms of our worship practices. It is deeply formative to actually physically gather, as fully embodied humans, in worship every week. To pray and laugh and weep together in small groups; to stand side by side and sing the same old songs, to sit and hear an actual pastor, in the flesh, preaching from a sacred text, rather than consuming content from a moving figure on a video. All of it—from the off-key notes of your pew mate to the public reading of Scripture to the lifting of the Communion cup—are subversive acts of protest against a world of chaos and spectacle, a formative spiritual rhythm that prepares you for life in the world.

I especially think these rituals are important for our kids. And I deliberately am using the word *rituals* here, because for so long evangelicals have communicated that we are all about relationship over ritual. There is some truth to that, as we are proclaiming the necessity of regeneration over and against a nominal faith that doesn't save. But we also need the rituals. We need the weekly coming to church, and the daily reading of the Word, and the repeated times of prayer. I often hear parents say, "I don't want Jesus to become a ritual for my kids." And I always want to stop and shake them and say,

"Yes, you do!" Humans are habitual creatures formed by ritual. If church and prayer and Jesus are not rituals for our kids, something else will be. Something, somewhere is catechizing your children—perhaps the content on their phones—so why not prioritize the formation that shapes them for worship?[3]

I also wonder if media saturation might cause us to rethink how we do youth ministry. I am not, by any means, an expert here. But it strikes me that what our kids don't need is more technology when they gather, but embodied, physical worship and deep social interaction. Because it could very well be that for many who walk into the doors of the church, this time is the only time in the week engaging in relationships is not mediated by a screen.

Your Podcast Is Not Your Pastor

We should also recognize the way the digital revolution is shaping the body of Christ. If you have access to the internet, you can experience a historically unprecedented and seemingly endless supply of Christian content. The internet has made it possible to access sermons on every part of the Bible from just about every Christian tradition, theological resources that would make the scholars of any previous era jealous, and low-cost or free resources from the most important figures in church history.

As someone who has benefited enormously from this rich feast, I believe we are in a great age. I love living in the twenty-first century. I have been shaped and formed by voices that I would not have known were it not for the internet. At key times in my life, God used the gifts of other brothers and sisters, some of whom I've never even met, to disciple my soul. When I was emerging out of an unhealthy church environment, it was *Christianity Today*'s daily "weblog" that helped point me to news about the wider, worldwide body of Christ. When I was looking for models of ministry and trying to learn and understand theology as a young pastor, organizations such as The Gospel Coalition, Redeemer Presbyterian Church, and Southern Baptist Theological Seminary helped shape my theological convictions. I am deeply grateful for the countless sermons from seminary chapels, theological lectures on iTunes, audiobooks, live conferences, and other content.

But as helpful as these things are, none of them can replace the church. I also owe much of my career and calling to the opportunities afforded me in this digital age. Online platforms and social media have allowed my work to be widely read and discovered. Of course, there were publishing opportunities before the internet, but the field expanded exponentially as content has been democratized. I'm glad that I'm able to discover and platform new authors, new writers, new voices that both shape my Christian life and allow me to nurture the faith of others in my local church and in my family.

And yet, in an age of spiritual abundance, with digital riches so readily available, we must not neglect the priority of the local church. There is a very present danger in allowing the internet to serve as a pseudo-church. Some have even championed a kind of internet church that features the excellence of digital content without the messiness of real-life church. This might be good for those with serious disabilities or perhaps as a gateway to the gathering of God's people commanded in Scripture. But if we can, we must keep gathering. We must not make screens and downloads our only or even our primary spiritual formation.

I'm guessing, if you are reading this, you have not gone to the extreme of doing church solely online. But there is another, subtler way we let the internet be our church. Because conferences and podcasting allow us to hear the most gifted expositors from around the globe during the week, we are tempted to judge our pastor's weekly preaching over and against the Christian celebrity preachers. But our podcasts cannot be our pastor. The guy I hear on Tuesday from a church a thousand miles away is not going to be at the bedside when my child is sick or is not going to counsel me when my marriage is in trouble. But my pastor will be there. And while your pastor may not have the rhetorical gifts of David Platt or the incisive analytical skills of Tim Keller or the exegetical prowess of John Piper, he is the one God has called to lead your congregation at this moment. Not only is it unfair to judge your pastor by your podcast, it's a distortion of what God intended for life in the local body.

Similarly, we may be tempted to judge the worship music at our churches over and against Christian celebrity worship artists. But again, Spotify cannot be our worship leader. While listening to excellent worship music can nourish our devotion, it's not realistic to expect twenty or ten or two moderately talented musicians in our congregation to deliver the kind of professional excellence offered by full-time, classically trained, auto-tuned musicians recording in New York and Nashville studios. Not only is it not realistic, it's not good, for there's something about sitting under even the flawed leadership of our worship leaders and hearing the off-key singing from the pew behind us that reminds us of the diversity of the body of Christ and our need of a Savior.

We can also allow the radical "purity" of our internet tribes to keep us from appreciating congregational life in our messy local assemblage of believers. I'm distressed, frankly, at the way tribalism has, in some ways, taken over evangelicalism. We seem to be in a moment not unlike what Paul was rebuking in 1 Corinthians 3:4, where the people of God were sorting themselves based on personality and style. Today we might reinterpret this passage to read something like, "I am of Beth Moore," or, "I am of N. T. Wright," or, "I am of Franklin Graham."

It's not at all bad to have theological preferences and favorite teachers. I could give you a list of the people whose work I read regularly, who shape me in unbelievable ways. But if we are not careful, we will forget that even the best of our teachers and preachers are mere humans and that life in the body of Christ means gathering weekly with people who might think differently, who might have differing views on the nonessentials, and who might favor styles that differ from ours. If we are so tethered to our preferred tribe, we'll not be able to obey God's command to live in biblical community together. We need to hold our tribes loosely.

In the same ways that the internet has been so beneficial to the body of Christ, helping us find good, sound theological resources, it has also been a sort of catalyst for tribalism. People who agree, even on the most tertiary issues of faith and practice, can easily find each other, form a community, and host content and conferences. This is helpful until it becomes harmful to community life, when our preferences become our identity in such a way that we set ourselves over and against other similarly preferential Christian communities. The internet rewards pugilism and clickbait-fueled suspicion. It doesn't reward unity across tribes. But Christians should resist these perverse incentives both in our online interactions with other Christians and in the way we approach body life. Consider Paul's words to the church at Colossae:

> Therefore, as God's chosen ones, holy and dearly loved, put on compassion, kindness, humility, gentleness, and patience, bearing with one another and forgiving one another if anyone has a grievance against another. Just as the Lord has forgiven you, so you are also to forgive. Above all, put on love, which is the perfect bond of unity. And let the peace of Christ, to which you were also called in one body, rule your hearts. And be thankful. (Col. 3:12–15)

Notice Paul urges the people of God to "put on" virtues such as compassion, kindness, humility, gentleness, and patience. He does this knowing that a local body of believers in Colossae and in any other community is inevitably made up of people who are at various stages of spiritual growth, who have varying convictions on lesser issues of faith and practice, and who have personalities that might occasionally grate against the other. We will also sin against each other in body life and must practice forbearance. This is not, of course, referring to egregious sins of abuse or heresy or financial malfeasance. In other passages Paul urges local bodies to practice church discipline for the health of the congregation and the witness of the church (1 Cor. 5). But for most of our garden-variety hurts and insults, Paul urges forgiveness and grace, lived out in community. Why? Because we are the chosen people of God.

Should we consume content from denominational and parachurch ministries? Should we read, download, and consume Christian content online? Of course! Otherwise I wouldn't be producing articles and podcasts and working for Christian organizations that publish. And as a pastor, I'm reliant on and regularly introducing good resources for our people. But we need to think about the way tribal affiliations, tertiary preferences, and favorite teachers influence our attitude toward our local church.

If we are not careful, we might allow ourselves to become "churched" more by those resources we enjoy *outside* our congregation and miss out on the embodied community life that God desires *within* our congregation. Brett McCracken, who works for The Gospel Coalition, urges his readers to not consider TGC their church. He says, "Christianity is not merely content. It's an embodied, lived community."[4]

For all the benefits offered by the glut of resources available in this age of "theological affluence," they cannot draw you out of yourself and into an embodied, others-oriented community. Websites like The Gospel Coalition offer a lot of (hopefully valuable!) resources to Christians, but they can't give you community in the way a local church can. They can't give you the communion elements or the experience of singing together and praying for one another week in and week out. TGC is not a church replacement. No online resource or parachurch ministry is.[5]

This is so true and something those of us who work for parachurch ministries or who are engaged in online discussions should remember. Our first loyalty should be to our local church. We should not measure our pastor's performance by our favorite podcast. We should not be frustrated but rather relieved when the members of our small group know nothing of the last fifteen Twitter controversies. And we should welcome the opportunity to grow by engaging in body life with people who have differing views on issues that are important but not primary.

In other words, are we willing to love those who might vote differently, who disagree with our eschatology, and whose liturgical preferences grate against our nerves? If not, it could be that we are allowing our preferred voices a place of authority that conflicts with God's design for the local church.

Hating on the Church

A commitment to faithful embodied church life should also temper the perverse incentives we find to rage against the church online. I want to be cautious here because I do think there is much for us to hear and learn from critics of both local churches and the worldwide body of Christ. Every generation sees, I believe, Spirit-directed, God-blessed reform movements that purify Christ's bride and call Christians to greater faith.

For instance, I'm deeply thankful for the way that courageous leaders rallied my own denomination toward a more faithful orthodoxy over and against a liberal, heterodox drift in the 1980s and 1990s. I'm also thankful for leaders like Martin Luther King Jr., whose prophetic ministry awakened the consciences of white pastors who, by their silence, were complicit in the systemic racism that kept black Americans in a perpetual state of virtual slavery. I'm grateful for the Protestant Reformation, for the revivals that have swept through the church throughout the ages, and for the recent Reformed resurgence that has impacted me so personally.

In recent years, digital platforms have, in many ways, given oxygen to important movements to reform the church. Yet easy access to these platforms has also created many perverse incentives to adopt a kind of performatively negative posture. Most days on social media seem like open season on Christ's bride, with a variety of voices slamming faithful people, churches, and movements for one offense or another. Some critiques are helpful. But many seem like signaling to a particular tribe, a way of ingratiating ourselves to those from whom we want approval. In fact, I dare say it's highly unpopular to go online and praise the church, the body for whom Christ gave his life.

This isn't to say we should be afraid to offer or even hear critiques, but we should ask ourselves, before writing that seemingly prophetic post, if we are genuinely interested in the purity of Christ's bride or we are just trying to make a name for ourselves. I'm also a bit nervous about critiques of "the church" as if there is one monolithic church that is all going in one specific way. The truth is that the worldwide church is unbelievably diverse, with pockets of problems and promise depending on the context, the leadership, and the plethora of movements and denominations. And none of us making our critiques is making them with full knowledge of every congregation or even most congregations. Even those of us who travel and minister to a variety of churches have probably only interacted with a small percentage of the body of Christ. So even using terms like, "Most churches . . ." or, "most pastors . . ." is not really used in good faith.

We can also grow cynical and lose sight of what God is doing among his people. The same God who led his people out of Egypt and out of the wilderness is alive today among his people. The same Jesus who defeated sin, death, and the grave is alive today. The same Spirit who forged a worldwide movement out of a ragtag band of scared disciples is alive today. The survival of God's people is not dependent on our ability to survive but is an eschatological fact backed up by Christ's own promise: "I will build my church, and the gates of Hades will not overpower it" (Matt. 16:18).

Christ *is* building his church. The gates of hell *will not* prevail against it. So while we need critique and we should fight heresy and lament abuse and work for reform, let's not lose sight of the end: God is gathering a people for himself and his kingdom. Our failures and foibles and faithlessness will not deter that, nor will our spiteful, critical words ensure it.

But you would not always get that impression by reading Christian Twitter or discernment bloggers or the many "gotcha" sites. You'd think that we are one scandal, one bad Christian movie, one story away from extinction. The church may recede or lose her voice in some parts of the world. Many churches may die in future generations. But the body of Christ will continue until Jesus returns. We may be wringing our hands online about the future of the church, but God is not in heaven wringing his.

This doesn't mean we should resist hearing or making prophetic pronouncements, but we should also temper our critiques with a love for the bride of Christ. Jesus loves his bride, and it's hard to imagine following Jesus in obedience and faith while regularly inflicting rhetorical wounds on the one for whom he died.

To Gather

A few years ago a prominent evangelical author declared that he was quitting church and would do spiritual formation on his own by consuming Christian content readily available without church. His critique is that church was, to him, nothing more than a TED Talk with music. He could likely find better Christian content and a better band online.

Thankfully, there were quite a few critiques of his decision to skip church on Sundays, but underneath his bad theology is the longing, I believe, for what the church can be.

If the local church is only that—the presentation of content and entertainment—the leavers are right. You will always find better exposition of the text from a more polished pastor or scholar online than you will find in your local context. You will undoubtedly find better worship music online. But what you will not find online is what God promises to do when his people gather in embodied worship:

> "For where two or three are gathered together
> in my name, I am there among them." (Matt.
> 18:20)

So let's gather, let's worship, let's find joy in what God is doing among his people. Christian content is good and vital for Christian discipleship. We should rejoice that this present age of innovation has made this possible. But let's remember that the church is not the sum of her content. The church is a Spirit-created, divinely crafted organism. We are the people, not the pixels, of God.

Chapter 10

The Internet for Good

*He has made everything appropriate in
its time. He has also put eternity in their
hearts, but no one can discover the work
God has done from beginning to end.*
—Ecclesiastes 3:11

I receive a fair amount of feedback from my articles, books, and podcasts—some positive, some negative, some plain crazy. But occasionally something comes in that takes my breath away. Today was one of those days.

But first, a little backstory: In the spring of 2016 I was approached at an Easter egg hunt (at my church, of all places) by a person who passionately disagreed with my opinion and the opinion of one of my very public colleagues regarding the 2016 election. I had never met this person before, who happened to be at our church because she was in town visiting relatives, who are members.

She really let me have it. And I vainly tried to explain my position while also trying to extricate myself from this awkward conversation in the middle of a bunch of people waiting for the Easter egg hunt to start. Her relatives were mortified and apologized profusely to me. I was fine and actually quite amused. I have a pretty thick skin and grew up in a family that encouraged strong disagreement. I had all but forgotten this incident until I received this email today.

Her note was kind and gracious and openhanded. She began by apologizing for the Easter incident and telling me that she had changed her mind about me, mostly because she followed me on Twitter and began reading my articles and books. She said that she thought I was always fair, even if she disagreed with me.

I wrote her back thanking her for such a kind email and admitted my own lack of civility at times, especially in the way I engaged the 2016 election and disparaged those who disagreed with my opinions. I told her I was writing a book on this topic and thanked her for her humility in being willing to mend fences.

Why am I sharing this story? I want you, the reader, to end this book feeling better about Christians and the giant network of tubes and pixels and wires and waves that makes up the internet. Despite all of the ways social media platforms seem to incentivize incivility, there are real opportunities to plant seeds of hope. The interwebs can take, but they can also give. And we can be part of what's true and beautiful online, if only we commit to it.

One of my favorite Twitter follows is "Church Curmudgeon." Whoever runs this account (and I have some hunches that I will not disclose at this moment) provides comic relief on Twitter with its exaggerated but true cranky takes on church life. And yet as much as I enjoy Church Curmudgeon, I don't want to emulate this posture when it comes to the digital age. I want, instead, to be hopeful.

The Internet for the Gospel

I had the opportunity recently to tour the new Museum of the Bible in Washington, DC, designed and built by the Green Family, owners of Hobby Lobby. I am usually very skeptical about Christian theme parks and their potential for mediocrity. But this museum is different, a world-class exhibition of the Bible curated by leading scholars. The museum tells the story of the Bible and its impact on history and culture, but perhaps the most affecting exhibit, for me, was a small, circular room that featured the work of the Illuminations Project. The room is filled, floor to ceiling, with colorful books. Each represents a specific people group. I noticed the large section of yellow books and asked the curator what these represented. He told me that these were the people groups without a version of the Bible in their own language.

The visual of this reality gave me pause. In my personal library I can count dozens of Bibles. Lying around our home are dozens more. And somewhere under pews and in Sunday school classrooms at church are still more of our personal copies of God's Word. I've never gone a day without having access to the Bible in multiple formats and translations. I can read a paper Bible. I can Google specific verses of the Bible. I can listen to audio versions of the Bible. But for too many people around the world, there is not any way they can interact with Scripture.

But this may not be the case for very long. New technologies are making the work of translation much easier and faster. This translation room at the Museum of the Bible highlights the work of a collaboration of Bible translation organizations, Illuminations. This new collective harnesses the most modern digital technologies and the power of the connectivity of the internet to share resources and advance the work of getting the Bible into the hands of every people group.

As of this writing, 3,879 languages still don't have a copy of God's Word, but project organizers estimate that by 2033 100 percent of people groups will have access to some portion of the Bible and 99.96 percent will have access to the entire New Testament. Because of the presence of shared digital libraries, artificial intelligence, and the ability to communicate across continents in real time, translation work has been reduced significantly.[1] There is also special software that allows texts to be analyzed side by side with the original, helping translators find word usage and translation errors and helping shepherd a translation from start to finish.[2]

I'm a layman when it comes to translation, so I can't even fully understand, let alone communicate to you, the way the digital age has made the process easier. But one thing is clear: the spread of God's Word is being helped by advances in technology.

In the previous chapter I lamented the way we often replace the printed text of Scripture with the Bible app, but we should celebrate the way the internet has allowed the spread of Scripture throughout the world, breaking down economic and social barriers. Consider the most popular Bible app, YouVersion, created out of a local church, Life. Church, in Oklahoma. As of this writing, almost 400 million users had installed the app on their phone and 227 million had completed a Bible reading plan. This app is available in every country on the globe and in forty-two languages.[3]

As a child I remember reading the heroic stories of Brother Andrew and others who risked their lives sneaking copies of the Bible behind the Iron Curtain. Today, even in closed countries, technology allows the Bible to get beyond political and social boundaries. Bible apps also allow elderly communities to read the Bible in a font that is readable and feature audio versions that can help blind or dyslexic folks engage God's Word in ways unavailable to previous generations.

This is just one of thousands of ways human flourishing is advancing in this time of rapid technological change, especially for Great Commission purposes. Consider how video chat services and inexpensive internet service allow missionaries to communicate with their sending churches and military service members to see and talk to their kids while away on deployment. Consider how social media has given us new ways to fundraise for important causes. These are just a few ways—even in a fallen world where thorns and thistles make our work more difficult and where sin easily corrupts—that God's redeemed image-bearers are obeying the mandate to create and innovate for his glory.

So while we should heed the warnings and beware of the pitfalls of the internet, we should not waste time wishing we lived in a bygone era. We should not long for the 1950s or the 1850s or the 1050s. God has planted us here, in this age, to live out his kingdom purposes. He is not, at this moment, wringing his hands over the internet.

Redeeming the Internet

This is why I cringe a little bit when well-meaning Christians want to totally write off the promise of the digital age. As we've seen, it's foolish to uncritically embrace every new innovation, but it's also foolish to condemn every new innovation. And in many ways, our laments about the internet are not laments about pixels and bytes and cables and screens but laments about the human condition, the worst of which is just newly exposed because of new communication tools. The internet is us. So rather than writing off social media and other platforms as irredeemable, let's be intentional about creating and communicating truth and beauty with the tiny corner of the internet we control.

How do we do this? How do we steward our words and images well online? I think we first begin with another question: *How can I make the internet a better place? How can I make my corner of the internet a better place?* I can't control the trolls that make a sport of attacking public figures. I can't stop the cycle of shame that greets Twitter every morning with fresh objects of derision. But I can bring joy and humor, prophetic words and gentle grace.

We face this choice with every piece of content we choose to make public online, whether it's a tweet or a Facebook post or an article or a podcast. There is a temptation, especially for creators, to withdraw, to let the cynicism of the age stifle our creative gifts. But to create, to make something, is an act of rebellion against the darkness, a sliver of light that points to a better world.

This is why I do what I do. Sure, I like getting paid for books and articles and other pieces of content. And I enjoy meeting gifted people I bring onto my podcast for interviews. But I also create because I believe that by creating, I'm offering my feeble gifts to serve the church and love my neighbor.

If you are a creator of any kind, even if all you create is social media posts, you must do this too. The digital world needs more light, more hope, more grace. To be an image-bearer is not to sit on our gifts but to use them to create as our Creator creates. We can be the solution to an uncivil, ugly world of social media. Even when we speak up for the vulnerable or declare truth to a world of confusion, we can contribute to a better, more edifying internet.

We can also make the internet better by refusing to yield to the narcissism of the age. Even as we create, we can refuse to always cast ourselves as the hero of the story. As a public voice, the temptation to seek glory is a fierce one, but we must allow the Holy Spirit to work in us, to offer our gifts not as ways to bring ourselves praise but to serve others. One way I've tried to do this is to make it a point to use whatever small platform I have to elevate other voices whose work brings joy to my heart. If I've read a good book, I try to share it on social media so others can discover it. If I read a wonderful piece of journalism or listen to a compelling podcast, I try to make others aware of it so they can be similarly blessed.

You can do this too. Whether your online platform is large or small, don't make it all about you. Be free with your praise of others' work. Share good content and ideas widely. Lift up others.

Sharing others' work is a way to both attack the problem of pride and attention-seeking and a way of resisting the 24/7 temptation to be an angry rage-bot. One of my favorite practices is to send a nice email or direct message to an author after I've read their book, if only to let them know that the project that consumed a significant portion of their time and energy brought wonder and grace to someone like me. You would be surprised at how rare it is for creators to receive good words about their work and how a short note of encouragement can be a balm to their souls. So don't hesitate. The internet has made this easy to do, so why not make it a habit?

Building a Better Internet

We should also all try to take ourselves less seriously. I enjoy following people online who have the capacity to laugh at quirky and ridiculous news in a broken world and to laugh at themselves. There are times for seriousness, for prophetic statements and for mourning, but there is also a time for laughter and hilarity. Comedy, I'm coming to believe, is not a luxury but a necessary oil for the gears of life. To laugh is to heal, a life detox that flushes out tension and reinvigorates the soul.

If we Christians want the internet to be better, we can start by being the better internet we want to see. That sounds a bit cheesy, I know, like some saying from a digital fortune cookie. But even if you are serious about theology, as you should be, and even if you care deeply about truth and justice, as I do, it doesn't mean your brow has to be constantly furrowed. In other words, there is some fine medium between Joel Osteen and the church lady from *Saturday Night Live*.

Christians also need to be better at laughing at our own tribes. This is why I appreciate attempts at humor. Even if the satire hits a bit close, even if it makes me say, "Ouch!" If we truly believe that Christ is our sovereign King and has conquered sin, death, and the grave, we can take the issues seriously but take ourselves not so seriously. We can laugh. We can joke. We can share ridiculous GIFs and hilarious memes. And we can do so for the glory of God.

The Internet Is Not Real

So I just said the internet is us; and yet, in many ways, it is not us. What I mean is this: as important and helpful and frustrating and wild as social media can be, let's remember as we close this book that it is not all there is to life. Seriously.

I'm reminded of this every time I gather in church and hang out with people, very few of whom are arguing on Facebook or are up to speed on the latest controversy. I'm reminded of this when I interact with people who don't do what I do for a living, which is most of the rest of the world. The HVAC guy who fixes my furnace isn't on Twitter all day and doesn't know what we are arguing about. My kids' teachers are busy teaching and are blissfully ignorant of what an intemperate state senator in North Dakota may have just posted on Instagram.

So let's use the internet, let's engage social media, let's let the gospel shape our words, but let's also log off, step away, close the laptop, put the phone down. Take a walk. Hug your kids. Read your Bible. Kiss your spouse.

Remember that devices and downloads and platforms and products are mere tools to be used, not idols to be served.

> ## Appendix A
>
> # 10 Things the Bible Says about Our Speech

There are several truths about our speech we should consider from Scripture:

1. The Bible commends honest speech. Proverbs 6:17 names "a lying tongue" as one of the things God hates. The prophet Zechariah instructed God's people: "These are the things you mustl do: Speak truth to one another" (Zech. 8:16). Paul commands the new covenant people of Ephesus, "speak the truth, each one to his neighbor" (Eph. 4:25). Lying is a sin, the product of a fallen nature. Lying is the work of the enemy (John 8:44). So truthful speech is the sign of a redeemed heart.

2. The Bible commends truthful speech for rebuke. Faithful, Proverbs says, are the wounds of a friend (Prov. 27:6). Flattery is the tool, not of someone looking to deepen a relationship but to leverage proximity for personal gain (Prov. 29:5). God used the courage of the prophet Nathan to confront David over his sin with Bathsheba (2 Sam. 12:7). Jesus in Matthew 18 gives instructions on redemptive confrontation designed to restore a sinful brother into loving community (vv. 15–17). Paul considers this a sign of love, from one brother or sister, to another (Gal. 6:1).

3. The Bible commends public arguments against sin and heresy. Jesus very publicly, throughout the Gospels, confronted errant religious leaders. When the heart of the gospel message was at stake, Paul was unafraid to confront Peter publicly (Gal. 2:11). And much of the New Testament consists of public letters that contain stinging rebukes of sin. Paul says that polemics are not only important within the church, at times, but also without, as we are tasked with engaging the reigning worldview and presenting an alternative, biblical worldview (2 Cor. 10:4b–5).

4. The Bible seems to commend the appropriate use of satire and other forms of creative engagement. Elijah playfully taunted the false prophets of Baal (1 Kings 18:27). Jesus employed the use of parables, metaphors, and similes in communicating truth. Paul was often acerbic in his rebuke of the Corinthians. Sharply worded polemics, uplifting satire, and, at times, sarcasm, can be employed in a way that reflects faithful Christian witness. However, this must be done within the boundaries of what is considered civil and wise speech (see below).

5. The Bible commends civility and respect in speech. In the Scriptures, kindness, respect, and good manners are not simply "nice" things for certain people, but are considered Christian virtues. Peter, in a letter written to address the persecution and marginalization of Christians, exhorts God's people to be both courageous and civil (1 Pet. 3:15–16).

Peter also reminds us to treat every single human being with dignity (1 Pet. 2:17). In the Pastoral Epistles, you will notice that one of the cornerstone characteristics of qualified church leaders is gentleness (Titus 1; 1 Tim. 3).

6. The Bible commends wise and informed speech. The way we speak is an oft-repeated theme in Scripture. James devotes almost an entire chapter to the power of the tongue (James 3). Words have power. Words matter. Words can either be life-giving or life-crushing. King David prayed for a mouth that offered words that were "acceptable" in the sight of God (Ps. 19:14). Proverbs affirms the value of applying just the right word in the right moment (Prov. 25:11) and, like James, rebukes those who speak before thinking (James 1:19; Prov. 17:28; 29:20).

7. The Bible says that the mouth is a good barometer of the heart. Luke records Jesus' words: "A good person produces good out of the good stored up in his heart. An evil person produces evil out of the evil stored up in his heart, for his mouth speaks from the overflow of the heart" (Luke 6:45). Words are not neutral; they reflect either good or evil. Nobody can really say, "I didn't mean that." It's better to say, when we misspeak, "Those words come from an unsanctified part of my heart." What's more, speaking my mind may not reflect what is true or virtuous, because the Christian mind is in a constant state of needing to be renewed by the gospel (Rom. 12:2; 2 Cor. 10:4b–5).

8. The Bible commends the wisdom of not sharing everything with everyone all the time. Proverbs says trustworthy people keep confidential information confidential and it is a sign of low character to reveal secrets (Prov. 11:13). Later, Proverbs extols the "prudent man" who knows to keep information to himself and rebukes the "heart of fools [that speak] folly" (Prov. 12:23 ESV). Sharing everything all the time to anyone who listens is not a sign of "authenticity" but a sign of foolishness.

9. The Bible commends humility as a sign of grace. "God resists the proud, but gives grace to the humble"—this maxim is mentioned three times in Scripture (Prov. 3:34; James 4:6; 1 Pet. 5:5). What does this have to do with our speech? It tells us, I believe, that graceful, measured, civil speech is a sign of God's grace, while proud, boastful speech is a sign of God's resistance. Humility means speaking with recognition of our own fallenness. It means resisting the urge to speak out of turn. It means we have the self-awareness to know if we are the right person to speak on a particular issue at a particular time.

10. The Bible commends speech that edifies. Paul, writing to the Ephesians, says that Christians can either speak words that destroy or words that build, words that are given with a desire to build up the body of Christ or words that are wielded as carnal weapons of destruction (Eph. 4:29). There is a difference, even, between verbal and written engagement meant to crush and winsome polemics meant to inform or rebuke.

The content of Appendix A was originally published at ERLC.com.

How to Read the News

How can Christians read the news well? On the one hand, we should resist the urge to think we have to know and comment publicly on everything all the time. On the other hand, we can't love our neighbors as Jesus commanded us if we pretend nothing is happening. So what does Christian discernment about the news look like? Here are six questions to ask.

1. Do I Have the Whole Story? It's too easy to just scan a headline and think we know the whole story. Today we are long on skimming and short on actual details. But if we are indeed people who care about truth, we can't form opinions without getting all of the facts. This is where James's wise words to the first-century church apply, with a slight change for application: Let's be quick to listen to the whole story, slow to tweet, slow to outrage (James 1:19).

"If a headline is too good or too bad or too sensational to be true, it probably is."

2. Is the Writer and Media Outlet Trustworthy? Don't fall for clickbait headlines and deceptive copy that frame a story in ways that make the subject look bad. Watch out for all publications, including Christians ones, sadly, that are built on sensationalism and half-truths. If a headline is too good or too bad or too sensational to be true, it probably is. And even among more established media outlets, it's good to know which journalists and voices are fair and which ones are pushing an agenda.

3. Am I Willing to Read News from a Variety of Sources? If we are truly concerned about knowing and communicating, "whatever is true" (Phil. 4:8), we have to be willing to process the news without the lens of our biases. For instance, I'm a conservative. If I'm not careful, I'll only get news from conservative-leaning outlets. For progressives, this temptation is similar. We need to read a variety of sources, from a variety of perspectives. This doesn't mean we abandon core convictions but that we are willing to face and seek the truth, wherever it leads. It's also good, sometimes, to read longer-form articles and listen to podcasts to get a fuller sense of what is happening rather than relying on short and incomplete bursts of information.

4. Am I Willing to Hear Bad News about My Own Tribe? All of us are prone to a concept known as "confirmation bias." This is the tendency to believe the stories that tell the best news about our guy or our tribe and the worst news about the other guy and the other tribe. This is especially acute and growing worse in the ways we discuss politics online, as politics increasingly replaces religion as a source of meaning and purpose. Christians need to resist this, especially since, as Christians, we have already confessed our imperfections and sinful nature to God. We should be willing to acknowledge the fallibility of our own party or movement and willing to acknowledge the goodness of others in another party or movement. By the way, if we resist confirmation bias, it will keep us from the sensational clickbait-type content we mentioned above.

"Social media has a habit of compelling you to comment on every news story from every source."

5. Am I Qualified to Comment on This Issue? Social media has a habit of compelling you to comment on every news story from every source. But the reality is that commenting on every post isn't necessary. Sometimes it's okay to read news and refrain from posting our opinions. It's good to stay in our lanes of expertise. Proverbs 17:28 is a great verse for the social media age: "Even a fool is considered wise when he keeps silent—discerning, when he seals his lips."

6. Can I Say Something Constructive That Will Provoke a Healthy Conversation? Even if we have a good understanding of a news story, we should still ask ourselves if we are capable of adding to healthy public discourse. I'm amazed at how often we think cathartic rage-tweeting will convince someone to change their mind about an issue. I'm amazed at how often elite opinion-makers think that talking down to people will cause them to change their minds. This doesn't mean we should never employ strong language in speaking out against evil, but most of the time when we think we are being "prophetic," we are just acting angrily.

This isn't an exhaustive list, but perhaps these diagnostic questions can help Christians think wiser about reading and reacting to the news. It may keep us from just going along with the currents of social media where narratives and opinions are often formed with heated passions and few facts. It's important for followers of Jesus to be discerning with our news-media diet so we can accurately assess the world and more fully love our neighbors.

The content of Appendix B was originally published at LifeWayVoices.com.

Notes

Introduction: A Book about Words

1. Timothy Ward, *Words of Life: Scripture as the Living and Active Word of God* (Downers Grove, IL: IVP Academic, 2009), 23–25.

2. Ibid., 27.

3. I want to be very careful in saying that communicating is not all that makes us human. As I discussed at great length in *The Dignity Revolution*, every human bears God's image regardless of ability, cognitive or otherwise. But it is right to say that communicating, at least at a high creative level, is a distinctly human endeavor, a gift from the Creator to his most prized creation.

4. Alan Jacobs, *How to Think: A Survival Guide for a World at Odds* (New York: Currency, 2017), 82.

Chapter 1: Ever Learning, Never Arriving

1. Elisabeth Scott, "The Stress of Constantly Checking Your Phone," Verywell Mind, accessed July 12, 2019, https://www.verywellmind.com/constantly-checking-your-phone-4137954.

2. Hannah Anderson, *All That's Good: Recovering the Lost Art of Discernment* (Chicago: Moody Publishers, 2018), 26.

3. Jen Pollock Michel, *Surprised by Paradox: The Promise of "And" in an Either-Or World* (Downers Grove, IL: InterVarsity Press, 2019), 35.

4. Fear of Missing Out

5. David Zahl, *Seculosity: How Career, Parenting, Technology, Food, Politics, and Romance Became Our New Religion and What to Do about It* (Minneapolis: Fortress Press, 2019), 76.

6. Nicholas Carr, "Is Google Making Us Stupid?" *The Atlantic,* July 1, 2008, http://www.theatlantic.com/magazine /archive/2008/07/is-google-making-us-stupid/6868/.

7. Tony Reinke, *Competing Spectacles: Treasuring Christ in the Media Age* (Wheaton, IL: Crossway, 2019), 67.

8. I want to highly recommend Curt Thompson's book, *The Soul of Shame.* His powerful description of knowing and being known by God has really shaped the way I've begun to think about the ways we approach knowledge and our own identity.

Chapter 2: Slow to Tweet, Quick to Listen, Quick to Get the Whole Story

1. John Blake, "How an Internet Mob Falsely Painted a Chipotle Employee as Racist," CNN, accessed August 2, 2019, https://www.cnn.com/2019/05/25/us/false-racism-internetmob -chipotle-video/index.html.

2. Ibid.

3. Rod Dreher, "No Sympathy for the Devil," *The American Conservative,* accessed August 2, 2019, https://www.the americanconservative.com/dreher/no-sympathy-for-the-devil -demonic-trump-politics/.

4. Shahram Heshmat, "What Is Confirmation Bias?" *Psychology Today,* accessed August 3, 2019, https://www

.psychologytoday.com/blog/science-choice/201504/what-is
-confirmation-bias.

5. Alan Jacobs, *How to Think* (New York: Currency, 2017), 22.

6. Ben Sasse, *Them: Why We Hate Each Other—and How to Heal* (New York: St. Martin's Publishing Group, 2018), 82.

7. Andrew Sullivan, "America's New Religions," *Intelligencer*, December 7, 2018, http://nymag.com/intelligencer/2018/12/andrew-sullivan-americas-new-religions.html.

8. David Zahl, *Seculosity: How Career, Parenting, Technology, Food, Politics, and Romance Became Our New Religion and What to Do about It* (Minneapolis: Fortress Press, 2019), 69.

9. Arthur C. Brooks, *Love Your Enemies: How Decent People Can Save America from the Culture of Contempt* (New York: HarperCollins, 2019), 146.

10. Matt Lewis, "Buzzfeed. Covington Catholic. Can We Ever Go 24 Hours without Having an Instant Freakout Over Something?" *The Daily Beast*, January 22, 2019, sec. politics, https://www.thedailybeast.com/buzzfeed-covington-catholic-can-we-ever-go-24-hours-without-having-an-instant-freakout-over-something.

11. David French, "Covington Catholic & Brett Kavanaugh—Covington School Is the Terrible Sequel to the Kavanaugh Case," *National Review*, accessed August 3, 2019, https://www.nationalreview.com/2019/01/covington-catholic-is-the-terrible-sequel-to-the-kavanaugh-case/.

Chapter 3: Biting and Devouring

1. Hannah Anderson, *All That's Good: Recovering the Lost Art of Discernment* (Chicago: Moody Publishers, 2018), 13.

2. Ibid., 27.

3. I'm thankful for my friend Thabiti Anyabwile for compiling this helpful list: "A Sampling of Paul's Instruction Re: False Teachers and Sound Doctrine," The Gospel Coalition (blog), accessed August 9, 2019, https://www.thegospelcoalition.org /blogs/thabiti-anyabwile/a-sampling-of-pauls-instruction-re -false-teachers-and-sound-doctrine/.

4. Arthur C. Brooks, *Love Your Enemies: How Decent People Can Save America from the Culture of Contempt* (New York: HarperCollins, 2019), 29.

5. Tim Challies, "In the Crosshairs of the Discernment Bloggers," (blog), April 3, 2013, https://www.challies.com /articles/in-the-crosshairs-of-the-discernment-bloggers/.

6. Kevin DeYoung is very helpful here in his short blog post: "Distinguishing Marks of a Quarrelsome Person," The Gospel Coalition (blog), accessed August 23, 2019, https://www.thegospelcoalition.org/blogs/kevin-deyoung /distinguishing-marks-quarrelsome-person/.

7. Challies, "In the Crosshairs of the Discernment Bloggers."

8. Thomas Schreiner, "Beware Theological Dangers on Both Left and Right," The Gospel Coalition (blog), accessed August 30, 2019, https://www.thegospelcoalition.org/article /orthodoxy-dangers-left-right/.

9. Jen Pollock Michel, *Surprised by Paradox : The Promise of "And" in an Either-Or World* (Downers Grove, IL: InterVarsity Press, 2019), 131.

Chapter 4: You Shouldn't Be Teachers

1. Michael Hyatt, "Four Temptations Christian Leaders Face," accessed July 19, 2019, https://michaelhyatt.com/four -temptations-christian-leaders-face/.

2. Ligon Duncan, "Some Thoughts on Social Media in Today's Culture and Climate," Reformed Theological Seminary,

accessed July 19, 2019, https://rts.edu/resources/some-thoughts
-on-social-media-in-todays-culture-and-climate/.

3. Paul D. Miller, "Faith and Healthy Democracy," released
September 2019, https://erlc.com/resource-library/white-papers
/faith-and-healthy-democracy.

4. Rod Dreher, "Trump Summons Demons," *The
American Conservative*, accessed August 2, 2019, https://
www.theamericanconservative.com/dreher/trump-summons
-demons-ilhan-omar/.

5. Thabiti Anyabwile, "Errata: An Apology to Some
Evangelicals," The Gospel Coalition (blog), accessed August
2, 2019, https://www.thegospelcoalition.org/blogs/thabiti-any
abwile/errata-apology-some-evangelicals/.

6. Kirsten Powers, "Kirsten Powers: I'm Not Proud of Role I've
Played in Toxic Public Debate. I Plan to Change.," *USA TODAY*,
accessed August 2, 2019, https://www.usatoday.com/story
/opinion/2019/02/19/kirsten-powers-covington-apology
-twitter-franken-social-media-toxic-column/2915856002/.

7. Alan Jacobs, *How to Think* (New York: Currency, 2017),
25.

8. Stefan Wojcik and Adam Hughes, "How Twitter Users
Compare to the General Public," Pew Research Center, accessed
August 3, 2019, https://www.pewinternet.org/2019/04/24/sizing
-up-twitter-users/.

9. Wendy Alsup on Twitter, accessed August 3, 2019, https://
twitter.com/WendyAlsup/status/1157646298050387968.

Chapter 5: More Highly Than We Ought

1. Kristen Bahler, "'Life in Those Squares Is Not Actually
Real.' Instagram Moms Are on a Quest for Wealth and Fame—But
at What Cost?" *Money*, accessed August 16, 2019, http://money.
com/money/5643889/instagram-mom-influencers-money-paid/.

2. Ibid.

3. Maggie Parker, "Honeymoon Hashtag Hell," *New York Times*, June 19, 2019, sec. Fashion, https://www.nytimes.com/2019/06/19/fashion/weddings/honeymoon-hashtag-hell.html.

4. Tony Reinke, *Competing Spectacles: Treasuring Christ in the Media Age* (Wheaton, IL: Crossway, 2019), 21.

5. David Zahl, *Seculosity: How Career, Parenting, Technology, Food, Politics, and Romance Became Our New Religion and What to Do about It* (Minneapolis: Fortress Press, 2019), xv.

6. D. A. Carson, *The Cross and Christian Ministry* (Grand Rapids: Baker Books, 1993), 31.

7. Zahl, *Seculosity*, xvi.

Chapter 6: Act Justly, Love Mercy, Post Humbly

1. "Alyssa Milano on Twitter: 'If You've Been Sexually Harassed or Assaulted Write "Me Too" as a Reply to This Tweet. Https://T.Co/K2oeCiUf9n' / Twitter," Twitter, accessed August 23, 2019, https://twitter.com/alyssa_milano/status/919659438700670976.

2. Raleigh Sadler, *Vulnerable: Rethinking Human Trafficking* (Nashville: B&H Publishing Group, 2019), 80–81.

3. Arthur Brooks, *Love Your Enemies: How Decent People Can Save America from the Culture of Contempt* (New York: HarperCollins, 2019), 51.

4. Talia Lakritz, "5 GoFundMe Campaigns That Weren't What They Claimed to Be," INSIDER, accessed August 23, 2019, https://www.thisisinsider.com/gofundme-campaign-scam-2018-12.

5. Mike Cosper, *Faith Among the Faithless: Learning from Esther How to Live in a World Gone Mad* (Nashville: Thomas Nelson, 2018), 84–85, 88.

6. Alanna Vagianos, "The 'Me Too' Campaign Was Created by a Black Woman 10 Years Ago," *HuffPost*, https://www.huffpost.com/entry/the-me-too-campaign-was-created-by-a-black-woman-10-years-ago_n_59e61a7fe4b02a215b336fee.

7. Sadler, *Vulnerable*, 55.

8. Skye Jethani, *With: Reimagining the Way You Relate to God* (Nashville: Thomas Nelson, 2011), 102.

Chapter 7: Whatsoever Is True

1. Tom Nichols, *The Death of Expertise: The Campaign Against Established Knowledge and Why It Matters* (New York: Oxford University Press, 2017), 58.

2. Albert Mohler, "How Should Christians Respond to Conspiracy Theories?" Ask Anything Live, 2019, https://www.youtube.com/watch?v=EiGJJeTyye0.

3. Ibid.

4. Ben Sasse, *Them: Why We Hate Each Other—and How to Heal* (New York: St. Martin's Press, 2018), 79.

5. Nichols, *The Death of Expertise*, 55.

6. As quoted by Justin Taylor, "The Vanity of Conspiracy Theories and the Banality of Real Evil," The Gospel Coalition (blog), accessed September 6, 2019, https://www.thegospelcoalition.org/blogs/justin-taylor/the-vanity-of-conspiracy-theories-and-the-banality-of-real-evil/.

7. Ed Stetzer, "Christians, Repent (Yes, Repent) of Spreading Conspiracy Theories and Fake News—It's Bearing False Witness," *The Exchange*, accessed September 6, 2019, https://www.christianitytoday.com/edstetzer/2017/may/christians-repent-conspiracy-theory-fake-news.html.

8. Ibid.

9. As quoted in Taylor, "The Vanity of Conspiracy Theories and the Banality of Real Evil."

10. Nichols, *The Death of Expertise*.

Chapter 8: As Much as Possible

1. Aimee Blanchette, "Families Divided in the Trump Era: 'I Didn't Talk to My Parents for Weeks,'" *Star Tribune*, accessed September 20, 2019, http://www.startribune.com /families-divided-in-the-trump-era-i-didn-t-talk-to-my -parents-for-weeks/415957734/.

2. Ben Sasse, *Them: Why We Hate Each Other—and How to Heal* (New York: St. Martin's Press, 2018), 128.

3. Kevin D. Williamson, *The Smallest Minority: Independent Thinking in the Age of Mob Politics* (New York: Simon & Schuster, 2019).

4. "The Hidden Tribes of America," Hidden Tribes, accessed September 20, 2019, http://hiddentribes.us.

5. As quoted in Paul D. Miller, "Faith and Healthy Democracy," Ethics and Religious Liberty Commission (ERLC), September 26, 2019, https://erlc.com/resource-library/ white-papers/faith-and-healthy-democracy.

6. Sohrab Ahmari, "Against David French-Ism," *First Things*, accessed September 27, 2019, https://www.firstthings .com/web-exclusives/2019/05/against-david-french-ism.

7. Robin Abcarian, "Must Reads: The Tender, Terrifying Truth about What Happened inside the Trader Joe's Hostage Siege," *Los Angeles Times*, accessed September 21, 2019, https:// www.latimes.com/local/la-me-abcarian-hostage-20180803 -story.html.

8. For a full treatment of this idea, please see Daniel Darling, *The Dignity Revolution: Reclaiming God's Rich Vision for Humanity* (Charlotte, NC: Good Book Company, 2018).

9. "Lethal Mass Partisanship: Prevalance, Correlates, and Electoral Contingencies," Nathan P. Kalmoe and Lilliana Mason, 2018.

10. © Stanford University, Stanford, and California 94305, "The American Dream," The Martin Luther King Jr., Research and Education Institute, July 3, 2014, https://kinginstitute.stanford.edu/king-papers/publications/knock-midnight-inspiration-great-sermons-reverend-martin-luther-king-jr-4.

11. Martin Luther King Jr., *A Testament of Hope: The Essential Writings and Speeches of Martin Luther King, Jr.* (New York: Harper Collins, 1990), 48.

12. Arthur Brooks, *Love Your Enemies: How Decent People Can Save America from the Culture of Contempt* (New York: HarperCollins, 2019), 51.

13. Check out the work of Curt Thompson, *Anatomy of the Soul: Surprising Connections between Neuroscience and Spiritual Practices That Can Transform Your Life and Relationships* (Carol Stream, IL: Tyndale House, 2010).

14. Andrew Sullivan, "America's New Religions," *Intelligencer*, December 7, 2018, http://nymag.com/intelligencer/2018/12/andrew-sullivan-americas-new-religions.html.

15. David Brooks, *The Second Mountain: The Quest for a Moral Life* (New York: Random House Publishing Group, 2019), 35.

16. David Zahl, *Seculosity: How Career, Parenting, Technology, Food, Politics, and Romance Became Our New Religion and What to Do about It* (Minneapolis: Fortress Press, 2019), 81.

17. James Mattis, "Duty, Democracy and the Threat of Tribalism," *Wall Street Journal*, August 28, 2019, sec. Life, https://www.wsj.com/articles/jim-mattis-duty-democracy-and-the-threat-of-tribalism-11566984601.

18. Trevin Wax, "The Words of the Christian Should Be Strong & Sweet," Trevin Wax (blog), accessed July 24, 2014, http://thegospelcoalition.org/blogs/trevinwax/2010/02/20/the-words-of-the-christian-should-be-strong-sweet/.

19. Miller, "Faith and Healthy Democracy."

Chapter 9: An Analog Church in a Digital Age

1. One of the best treatments of this is Gordon MacDonald, *Who Stole My Church: What to Do When the Church You Love Tries to Enter the 21st Century* (Nashville: Thomas Nelson, 2010). If you are leading a church through change, I strongly recommend it.

2. Jean M. Twenge, *iGen: Why Today's Super-Connected Kids Are Growing Up Less Rebellious, More Tolerant, Less Happy—and Completely Unprepared for Adulthood—and What That Means for the Rest of Us* (New York: Simon & Schuster, 2017), 88.

3. Time sadly permits me from expanding on this theme of habit and worship and ritual, but I feel it's so important. So, when you are finished with this book, kindly go read James K. A. Smith, *You Are What You Love: The Spiritual Power of Habit* (Grand Rapids: Brazos Press, 2016).

4. Brett McCracken, "Nothing on Your Phone (Including TGC) Can Replace the Local Church," The Gospel Coalition (blog), accessed October 2, 2019, https://www.thegospelcoalition.org/article/nothing-phone-tgc-local-church/.

5. Ibid.

Chapter 10: The Internet for Good

1. Sarah Eekhoff Zylstra, "Together for the Gospels," ChristianityToday.com, accessed October 18, 2019, https://www.christianitytoday.com/ct/2017/may/together-for-gospels-bible-translation-unity-illuminations.html.

2. "The Impact of Technology on Bible Translation | Lausanne World Pulse Archives," accessed October 18, 2019, https://www.lausanneworldpulse.com/themedarticles-php/1214/10-2009.

3. "YouVersion, The Bible App: End of the Year 2018," accessed October 18, 2019, https://share.bible.com/2018/.